>>> **Introduction**

Welcome to The Journey of Preparing for Python interviews.

Python has become one of the most important programming languages in the world, used in areas ranging from web development to data engineering.

Interviews for Python roles require a mix of practical skills, problem-solving abilities, and an understanding of how Python works at a deeper level.

This book is here to guide you through every step and help you build the confidence to excel in any Python interview.

The chapters are carefully organized to cover everything from the basics to advanced topics like asynchronous programming, Big Datas, AI, Data Engineering and cloud-based systems. You can start from the beginning and work through the book step by step or jump straight to the sections where you want to focus.

Python interviews aren't just about answering questions, they're about showing your understanding of the language, applying concepts in real-world scenarios, and communicating your solutions clearly. This book provides insights, examples, and explanations to prepare you for all these aspects and more.

Dive In, and let's get you ready for Python interviews that reflect the challenges and opportunities of today's tech world.

I wish you a Happy Reading and Good Luck to Your Job Interview!

You can contact me through the email address if you have any questions or suggestions regarding the book.

Please share with me me the results of your job interview as well as provide your feedback ☺ I would be happy to hear from you... ♡

Email: gleamixie@gmail.com

Please note the information contained within this document is for educational and entertainment purposes only. All effort has been executed to present accurate, up to date, reliable, complete information. No warranties of any kind are declared or implied. Readers acknowledge that the author is not engaged in the rendering of legal, financial, medical or professional advice.

>>> Specification

Python stands tall as one of the most impactful programming languages of the modern era. In 2025 and the years ahead, its role in shaping the digital world is more pivotal than ever. This book examines Python not just as a tool, but as a phenomenon - a driving force behind revolutionary advancements in AI, data engineering, and beyond.

More than that, it explores how Python transcends its technical capabilities to become a catalyst for innovation across industries. With its simplicity, adaptability, and global community, Python continues to empower millions of individuals, from experts solving complex problems to curious beginners taking their first steps into coding. As technology evolves, Python's influence persists, adapting and thriving in every new frontier.

By the way, this guide aims not only to prepare to the Python interview but also to inspire and equip readers to embrace the challenges and opportunities of the future, with Python as their ally. Whether you're building cutting-edge applications or shaping the world in imaginative ways, Python is a language of progress - a language of possibility.

>>> **Core Python Concepts**

Question 1 | Core Python Concepts

What is the significance of indentation in Python syntax ?

Answer

Indentation is a fundamental part of Python's syntax. Unlike other programming languages that use braces {} or keywords to define code blocks, Python uses indentation to signify hierarchical structures, such as loops, conditionals, and function definitions.

Points for Consideration

❖ Indentation levels must be consistent, mixing tabs and spaces causes errors.

❖ Indentation enhances readability, aligning with Python's philosophy.

" There should be one and preferably only one obvious way to do it."

Example Code

```python
x = 42

if x > 0:
    print("Positive number")  # Indented block
print("Outside the conditional")  # No indentation
```

Question 2 | Core Python Concepts

What does Pythonic mean, and how can code be Pythonic ?

Answer

'Pythonic' refers to writing code that adheres to Python's idiomatic style, emphasizing clarity, simplicity, and elegance. Pythonic code leverages built-in features and avoids unnecessarily complex constructions.

Characteristics of Pythonic Code

❖ Using list comprehensions instead of loops for creating lists.

❖ Embracing built-in functions like `zip()` or `enumerate()`.

❖ Writing readable and expressive code aligned with **The Zen of Python** (`import this`).

Non-Pythonic Example

```
result = []
my_list = [1, 2, 3, 4, 5] # Example list
for i in range(len(my_list)):
    result.append(my_list[i] * 2)
```

Pythonic Example

```
result = [x * 2 for x in my_list]
```

Question 3 | Core Python Concepts

What are docstrings, and how do they contribute to Python's syntax ?

Answer

Docstrings are multiline string literals used to document Python modules, classes, methods, or functions. They provide a clear description of the purpose and usage of the code.

The Main Features of Docstrings

❖ Enclosed in triple quotes (""" """).

❖ Accessible via `help()` for introspection.

Example Code

```python
def add(a, b):
    """
    Adds two numbers and returns the result.

    Parameters:
    a (int): First number
    b (int): Second number

    Returns:
    int: The sum of a and b
    """
    return a + b
```

Question 4 | Core Python Concepts

What is tuple unpacking ?

Answer

Tuple unpacking refers to assigning values from a tuple (or other iterable) directly to multiple variables in a single statement. This concise syntax aligns with Pythonic idioms.

Example Code

```python
coordinates = (10, 20)
x, y = coordinates   # Tuple unpacking
print(f"x: {x}, y: {y}")
```

Question 5 | Core Python Concepts

What is the difference between single quotes ' ' double quotes " " and triple quotes "'' ""' ?

Answer

The single quotes ' ' and double quotes " " are functionally identical for defining string literals. The main reason to choose one over the other is based on readability or the need to avoid escape characters.
The triple quotes "'' ''' are used for multi-line strings.

Question 6 | Core Python Concepts

What is the difference between implicit and explicit type conversion ?

Answer

Type conversion refers to changing a variable's type.

Implicit Conversion (Type Coercion) - Done automatically by Python when mixing compatible types.

```
num = 5     # Integer
result = num + 2.5   # Implicitly converted to float (7.5)
```

Explicit Conversion (Type Casting) - Done manually using built-in functions (int(), float(), str())

```
num = "42"
result = int(num) #Explicitly converted to an integer(42)
```

Question 7 | Core Python Concepts

What is the difference between shallow and deep copies ?

Answer

A shallow copy creates a new object but does not copy nested objects, meaning changes in the copy may affect the original.

A deep copy recursively copies all nested objects, ensuring complete independence.

Example Code

```python
import copy

original = [[1, 2], [3, 4]]
shallow = copy.copy(original)
deep = copy.deepcopy(original)

shallow[0][0] = 99  # This affects the original list
print(original)  # [[99, 2], [3, 4]]

deep[0][0] = 50  # This does NOT affect the original
print(original)  # [[99, 2], [3, 4]]
```

Question 8 | Core Python Concepts

What is the purpose of the pass statement ?

Answer

The pass statement is a no-op (no operation) placeholder used when a block of code is syntactically required but no action is needed. It allows the program to run without errors while the block is intentionally left empty.

Use Cases

❖ **Stub functions** - When defining a function that will be implemented later.

❖ **Placeholder for conditionals** - Where logic is not yet defined but needs syntactic correctness.

❖ **Empty class definitions** - When defining a class structure before adding attributes or methods.

Example Code

```python
def future_function():
    pass   # Function placeholder

for i in range(5):
    pass   # Loop runs, but does nothing
```

[!TIP] pass differs from None, None is a returnable object, whereas pass is purely syntactic.

Question 9 | Core Python Concepts

What is the difference between 'is' and == operators ?

Answer

❖ == **(Equality Operator)** - Compares the values of two objects to check if they are logically equal.

❖ is **(Identity Operator)** - Checks if two variables point to the same object in memory.

Example Code

```
a = [1, 2, 3]
b = [1, 2, 3]
c = a

print(a == b)   # True (values are the same)
print(a is b)   # False (different memory locations)
print(a is c)   # True (c is just another ref to a)
```

[!Tip] Misusing is for equality checks leads to subtle bugs. Use == unless checking identity explicitly.

Question 10 | Core Python Concepts

What is LEGB rule ?

Answer

The **LEGB (Local, Enclosing, Global, Built-in)** rule to determine variable scope

❖ **Local** - Inside the function where the variable is defined.

❖ **Enclosing** - In an enclosing function (nested function).

❖ **Global** - Defined at the module level, accessible throughout the script.

❖ **Built-in** - Predefined names like print, len, sum.

Example Code

```
x = "Global"

def outer():
    x = "Enclosing"

    def inner():
        x = "Local"
        print(x)  # Local scope takes priority

    inner()
    print(x)  # Enclosing scope

outer()
print(x)  # Global scope
```

Question 11 | Core Python Concepts

What are the different ways to format strings ?

Answer

Python supports multiple string formatting techniques.

❖ **Old-style** (% operator) - Not recommended due to readability issues.

❖ `.format()` method - More flexible and readable.

❖ **f-strings** (Recommended, Python 3.6+) - Fast and intuitive.

Example Code

```
# Using .format()
name = "Kevin"
print("Hello, {}!".format(name)) # Hello, Kevin!

# Using f-strings (Recommended)
age = 25
print(f"Name: {name}, Age: {age}") # Name: Kevin, Age: 25

# Using % (Legacy)
print("Price: %.2f" % 9.99) # Price: 9.99
```

[!TIP] Prefer f-strings for readability and performance over .format() and %.

Question 12 | Core Python Concepts

What is the difference between del, pop(), and remove() when working with lists ?

Answer

❖ **del** statement - Removes an item at a specified index or deletes an entire list.

❖ **pop()** method - Removes and returns an element at a given index; defaults to the last element.

❖ **remove()** method - Deletes a specified value from the list without returning it.

Example Code

```
numbers = [1, 2, 3, 4, 5]

del numbers[1] # RM index 1 → [1, 3, 4, 5]
print(numbers)

popped_value = numbers.pop(2) # RM index 2 → [1, 3, 5]
print(popped_value) # Prints 4

numbers.remove(3) # RM the value 3 → [1, 5]
print(numbers)
```

[!TIP] pop() is useful when modifying lists dynamically, while del is for direct deletion.

Question 13 | Core Python Concepts

What are keyword-only arguments ?

Answer

Keyword-only arguments enforce that certain parameters must be specified using named arguments instead of positional arguments. They are defined after the * in function definitions.

Example Code

```
def fetch_data(id, *, cache=False):
    print(f"Fetch data for ID {id} with cache={cache}")

fetch_data(42, cache=True)  # Correct usage
fetch_data(42, True)        # Error
```

Question 14 | Core Python Concepts

What is the difference between `if-elif-else` and `match-case` ?

Answer

- ❖ **if-elif-else** Statement - Executes conditional blocks based on Boolean expressions.

- ❖ **match-case** Statement (Python 3.10+) - Works similarly to switch-case in other languages, providing a cleaner way to handle multiple conditions.

Example Code

```python
# Traditional if-elif-else approach
def check_status(code):
    if code == 200:
        return "OK"
    elif code == 404:
        return "Not Found"
    else:
        return "Unknown"

# Using match-case (Python 3.10+)
def check_status(code):
    match code:
        case 200:
            return "OK"
        case 404:
            return "Not Found"
        case _:
            return "Unknown"
```

[!TIP] Use match-case for cleaner, more readable pattern matching when dealing with multiple conditions.

Question 15 | Core Python Concepts

What are custom exceptions ?

Answer

Custom exceptions allow developers to define meaningful error handling tailored to their application's logic.

Example Code

```python
class InvalidInputError(Exception):
    """Custom exception for invalid user input"""
    def __init__(self, message="Invalid input provided"):
        self.message = message
        super().__init__(self.message)

# Raising the custom exception
def process_input(value):
    if value < 0:
        raise InvalidInputError("Negatives not allowed")

try:
    process_input(-5)
except InvalidInputError as e:
    print(e)   # Outputs: Negative values are not allowed
```

Question 16 | Core Python Concepts

What is Global Interpreter Lock (GIL), and how does it affect multi-threading ?

Answer

The **Global Interpreter Lock** (GIL) is a mutex that prevents multiple native threads from executing Python bytecode simultaneously. This means that even in multi-threaded Python programs, only one thread can execute Python code at a time.

Effects on Multi-threading

- ❖ Limits true parallel execution in CPU-bound tasks (e.g. heavy computations).

- ❖ Does not affect I/O-bound tasks, where multi-threading can still be beneficial (e.g. network requests).

Workarounds for Parallelism

- ❖ Use multiprocessing to bypass the GIL by spawning separate processes.

- ❖ Utilize Cython or numpy for optimized parallel computations.

- ❖ Implement async programming (asyncio) for efficient I/O operations.

Question 17 | Core Python Concepts

What is the purpose of __init__.py file ?

Answer

The __init__.py file is used to mark a directory as a Python package, allowing the directory's contents to be imported as modules.

The main features are

- ❖ Defines package-wide initialization code.

- ❖ Can execute setup logic when the package is imported.

- ❖ May contain __all__ to control module imports.

Example Directory Structure

```
my_package/
├── __init__.py
├── module1.py
├── module2.py
```

Question 18 | Core Python Concepts

What is the difference between Python's list and tuple ?

Answer

❖ **List** - Mutable, can be modified after creation (append, pop, remove).

❖ **Tuple** - Immutable, cannot be changed after creation.

Performance Difference

❖ Tuples are faster than lists for iteration due to immutability.

❖ Tuples are hashable, meaning they can be used as dictionary keys.

Question 19 | Core Python Concepts

What is the purpose of Python's with statement ?

Answer

The with statement simplifies resource management by ensuring that resources like files or network connections are automatically cleaned up after use, even if an error occurs.

```python
with open("data.txt", "r") as file:
    content = file.read()   # No need for manual closing

# The file is automatically closed after the block
```

[!Tip] Use with for file handling, database connections, and threading locks to prevent resource leaks.

Question 20 | Core Python Concepts

What is the difference between @staticmethod and @classmethod ?

Answer

❖ **@staticmethod** - Defines a method that **does not** take any implicit parameters. (self or cls)

❖ **@classmethod** - Defines a method that takes the class (cls) as its first parameter.

Example Code

```python
class MyClass:

    @staticmethod
    def static_method():
        print("Static method called")

    @classmethod
    def class_method(cls):
        print(f"Class method called from {cls.__name__}")

MyClass.static_method()
MyClass.class_method()
```

[!Tip] Use @classmethod for **factory methods** or alternative constructors.

Question 21 | Core Python Concepts

What is the purpose of __repr__ method ?

Answer

The __repr__ method provides a developer-friendly string representation of an object, useful for debugging.

```python
class Person:

    def __init__(self, name): self.name = name

    def __repr__(self):
        return f"Person(name='{self.name}')"

p = Person("Mark") print(p) # Person(name='Mark')
```

Question 22 | Core Python Concepts

What is the difference between del and garbage collection ?

Answer

❖ del statement - Removes a reference to an object.

❖ **Garbage Collector** (gc module) - Automatically cleans up objects when no references remain.

Example Code

```
import gc

x = [1, 2, 3]
del x   # Deletes reference but does not force cleanup

gc.collect()   # Explicitly triggers garbage collection
```

[!Tip] Avoid manual garbage collection unless troubleshooting memory leaks.

Question 23 | Core Python Concepts

What is the purpose of __name__ variable ?

Answer

The __name__ variable stores the module name and determines whether a script is run directly or imported.

Example Code

```
if __name__ == "__main__":
    print("Script is running directly")
else:
    print(f"Imported as a module: {__name__}")
```

[!Tip] Always use if __name__ == "__main__" to prevent unintended execution when importing modules.

Question 24 | Core Python Concepts

What are dataclasses, and how do they improve code readability ?

Answer

Dataclasses (@dataclass) introduced in Python 3.7 simplify class creation by automatically generating methods like __init__(), __repr__(), and __eq__().

Example using dataclass

```python
from dataclasses import dataclass

@dataclass
class Person:
    name: str
    age: int

p1 = Person("David", 30)
print(p1)   # Person(name='David', age=30)
```

Advantages

❖ Reduces boilerplate code, no need to manually define __init__()
  and other methods.

❖ Automatic ordering and comparisons when adding order=True.

❖ Makes code cleaner and more maintainable.

Question 25 | Core Python Concepts

What is the difference between __str__ and __repr__ methods ?

Answer

❖ __str__ - Returns a user-friendly string representation of an object.

❖ __repr__ - Returns a developer-friendly representation meant for debugging.

Example Code

```python
class Demo:
    def __str__(self):
        return "User-friendly representation"

    def __repr__(self):
        return "Debugging representation"

obj = Demo()
print(str(obj))   # User-friendly representation
print(repr(obj))  # Debugging representation
```

[!Tip] __repr__ should return a valid Python expression that can recreate the object.

Question 26 | Core Python Concepts

What are @static_method and @class_method ?

Answer

❖ **Instance Methods** (`self`) - Operate on an object instance and can access instance attributes.

❖ **Class Methods** (`cls`) - Operate on the class itself rather than an instance, shared across all instances.

❖ **Static Methods** - Behave like regular functions but belong to a class.

Example Code

```python
class Example:
    def instance_method(self):
        return "Instance method called"

    @classmethod
    def class_method(cls):
        return f"Class method called from {cls.__name__}"

    @staticmethod
    def static_method():
        return "Static method called"

obj = Example()
print(obj.instance_method())

# Instance method called print(Example.class_method())
# Class method called from Example
# print(Example.static_method())
# Static method called
```

[!Tip] Use `@classmethod` for alternative constructors and `@staticmethod` for utility functions.

Question 27 | Core Python Concepts

What are map, filter and reduce methods ?

Answer

These **higher-order functions** apply operations across iterables efficiently.

- ❖ `map(function, iterable)` - Applies a function to each item in an iterable.

- ❖ `filter(function, iterable)` - Keeps only items where the function returns True.

- ❖ `reduce(function, iterable)` - Applies a rolling operation (from functools).

Example Code

```python
from functools import reduce

numbers = [1, 2, 3, 4]

mp = list(map(lambda x: x * 2, numbers)) # [2, 4, 6, 8]
fl = list(filter(lambda x: x % 2 == 0, numbers)) # [2, 4]
rd = reduce(lambda x, y: x + y, numbers) # 10
```

`[!Tip]` Prefer list comprehensions for `map()` and `filter()` in modern Python.

Question 28 | Core Python Concepts

What is memoization, and how can it optimize functions ?

Answer

Memoization caches previous computations to avoid redundant recalculations.

Example using lru_cache from functools

```python
from functools import lru_cache

@lru_cache(maxsize=100)
def fibonacci(n):
    if n < 2:
        return n
    return fibonacci(n - 1) + fibonacci(n - 2)

print(fibonacci(30)) # FIB using memoization
```

Use Cases

❖ **Optimizing recursive algorithms** (Fibonacci, pathfinding).

❖ **Reducing API/database calls** by caching previous results.

Question 29 | Core Python Concepts

What is monkey patching, and why should it be used cautiously ?

Answer

Monkey patching modifies methods or attributes of modules/classes dynamically at runtime.

Example of monkey patching a function

```python
class Demo:
    def original(self):
        return "Original method"

def patched(self):
    return "Patched method"

Demo.original = patched  # Monkey patch applied
print(Demo().original())  # Outputs: Patched method
```

Risks

❖ Can introduce unexpected behaviors or break functionality.

❖ Makes debugging difficult in large applications.

[!Tip] Use monkey patching only when absolutely necessary, such as modifying third-party libraries.

Question 30 | Core Python Concepts

What are frozen dataclasses, and how do they enforce immutability ?

Answer

Frozen dataclasses (`@dataclass(frozen=True)`) prevent attribute modification after creation.

Example Code

```python
from dataclasses import dataclass

@dataclass(frozen=True)
class Config:
    setting: str

config = Config("dark_mode")
config.setting = "light_mode"  # TypeError
```

Benefits

❖ Ensures data integrity (useful for configurations).

❖ Enables hashability, allowing usage as dictionary keys.

Question 31 | Core Python Concepts

What are weak references, and how do they improve memory management ?

Answer

Weak references (`weakref` module) allow referencing objects without increasing their reference count, enabling efficient garbage collection.

```python
import weakref

class MyClass:
    pass

obj = MyClass()
weak_ref = weakref.ref(obj)

print(weak_ref())   # Returns object reference
del obj
print(weak_ref())   # Returns None
```

[!TIP] Use weak references when caching temporary objects without preventing memory cleanup.

Question 32 | Core Python Concepts

What are Magic methods ?

Answer

Magic methods (dunder methods, e.g. __init__, __str__, __eq__) define object behavior for built-in operations.

```python
class Demo:
    def __init__(self, value):
        self.value = value

    def __str__(self):
        return f"Demo Object with value {self.value}"

    def __eq__(self, other):
        return self.value == other.value

obj1 = Demo(5)
obj2 = Demo(5)

print(str(obj1))    # Calls __str__
print(obj1 == obj2)  # Calls __eq__
```

Question 33 | Core Python Concepts

How does Python implement method resolution order (MRO), and why is it important ?

Answer

Python follows C3 linearization (MRO) to determine the sequence in which methods are inherited from multiple parent classes.

Example using super() in multiple inheritance

```python
class A:
    def greet(self):
        return "Hello from A"

class B(A):
    def greet(self):
        return super().greet() + " & B"

class C(B):
    def greet(self):
        return super().greet() + " & C"

obj = C()
print(obj.greet())   # Hello from A & B & C
print(C.__mro__)    # Shows method resolution order
```

Importance of MRO

❖ Prevents diamond inheritance issues.

❖ Ensures consistent method execution order.

Question 34 | Core Python Concepts

How does Python internally handle mutability, and what are its implications ?

Answer

Python handles mutability using object identity and reference counting.

❖ Mutable objects have a variable memory address, meaning modifications affect the object itself.

❖ Immutable objects are reallocated in memory upon change.

Example Code

```
x = "hello"
print(id(x))   # Memory address of x

x = x + " world" # Immutable update (new memory address)
print(id(x))   # Different memory address

y = [1, 2, 3]

print(id(y))   # Memory address of y
y.append(4)    # Mutable update (same memory address)
print(id(y))   # Same memory address
```

Question 35 | Core Python Concepts

What are Python's built-in functions ?

Answer

Built-in functions provide essential utilities without requiring external modules.

Examples

❖ **Type conversions** - int(), float(), str()

❖ **Data operations** - `len(), sum(), max(), sorted()`

❖ **Iterators** - `enumerate(), zip(), map(), filter()`

❖ **Functional programming** - `lambda, reduce()`

Question 36 | Core Python Concepts

Why should you avoid using a blanket except: clause, and what are the risks ?

Answer

Using a blank `except:` clause (without specifying exception types) catches all errors, including system interrupts.

Risks of Blanket Exception Handling

❖ **Hides real errors** - makes debugging harder.

❖ **Catches system exceptions** (KeyboardInterrupt, SystemExit) unintentionally.

❖ **Might suppress necessary failures**, leading to hidden bugs.

Best Practices

❖ Always specify exception types (`except ValueError:` instead of `except:`).

❖ Log errors properly rather than silently handling them.

❖ Use `except Exception:` only if catching all application-level errors is necessary.

>>> Artificial Intelligence (AI)

Question 37 | AI

How does Python enable generative AI for text, image, and code generation ?

Answer

Python provides libraries and frameworks that simplify generative AI tasks

- ❖ **Text Generation** - Libraries like transformers (Hugging Face) enable fine-tuning models like GPT for text generation.

- ❖ **Image Generation** - Tools like Stable Diffusion and DALL-E use Python APIs for generating high-quality images.

- ❖ **Code Generation** - Models like Codex (OpenAI) leverage Python for generating code snippets based on natural language prompts.

Why Python is Preferred

- ❖ **Ease of integration** - Python's ecosystem supports seamless integration with AI frameworks.

- ❖ **Community support** - Extensive documentation and active developer communities.

- ❖ **Versatility** - Python can handle preprocessing, model training, and deployment in a single pipeline.

Question 38 | AI

How does PyTorch framework simplify advanced machine learning tasks ?

Answer

PyTorch is a dynamic computation graph framework that allows flexibility in building and training models.

- ❖ **Ease of debugging** - PyTorch's dynamic graph enables real-time debugging during model execution.

- ❖ **Custom layers** - Python allows developers to create custom neural network layers using PyTorch's modular design.

- ❖ **Distributed training** - PyTorch supports distributed training across GPUs and TPUs, making it ideal for large-scale AI tasks.

Question 39 | AI

What are differences between PyTorch and TensorFlow ?

Answer

PyTorch

- ❖ **Dynamic computation graphs** - Easier debugging and experimentation.

- ❖ **Preferred for research** - Widely adopted in academia for prototyping.

- ❖ **Pythonic syntax** - Intuitive for Python developers.

TensorFlow

- ❖ **Static computation graphs** - Better for production environments.

- ❖ **TensorFlow Extended (TFX)** - Provides tools for end-to-end ML pipelines.

- ❖ **Cross-platform support** - Optimized for mobile and embedded devices.

Choosing Between Them

- ✓ Use **PyTorch** for research and experimentation.

- ✓ Use **TensorFlow** for production-grade applications requiring scalability.

Question 40 | AI

How does Python facilitate Natural Language Processing (NLP) with libraries like spaCy and NLTK ?

Answer

Python's NLP libraries provide tools for **text preprocessing**, **tokenization**, and **semantic analysis**.

- ❖ **spaCy** - Optimized for production-level NLP tasks like named entity recognition (NER) and dependency parsing.

- ❖ **NLTK** - Ideal for academic and research purposes, offering tools for text classification, stemming, and sentiment analysis.

Advantages of Python for NLP

- ❖ **Pre-trained models** - Libraries like spaCy include pre-trained pipelines for common languages.

- ❖ **Integration with deep learning** - Python allows seamless integration of NLP libraries with frameworks like PyTorch and TensorFlow.

- ❖ **Custom pipelines** - It is possible to create custom NLP pipelines for domain-specific tasks.

Question 41 | AI

What are the advantages of using FastAPI over Flask for AI model deployment ?

Answer

FastAPI Advantages

- ❖ **Asynchronous support** - Handles concurrent requests efficiently using **asyncio**.

- ❖ **Automatic validation** - Built-in support for request validation using **Pydantic**.

- ❖ **Performance** - Faster than **Flask** due to asynchronous capabilities.

When to Use Flask

- ❖ For simple applications with minimal concurrency requirements.

- ❖ When working with legacy systems that rely on Flask.

Question 42 | AI

How can Python engineers ensure transparency in generative AI models ?

Answer

Transparency can be achieved by

- ❖ **Documenting training data** - Clearly specify the sources and preprocessing steps.

- ❖ **Providing model explanations** - Use tools like **SHAP** to explain predictions.

- ❖ **Open-sourcing models** - Share code and datasets to allow peer review.

Question 43 | AI

How does Python support ethical AI development through libraries and frameworks ?

Answer

Python tools for ethical AI development

- ❖ **Fairlearn** - Mitigates bias in machine learning models.

- ❖ **AI Explainability 360** - Offers techniques for explaining model predictions.

- ❖ **Differential Privacy Libraries** - Ensure privacy in AI applications.

Question 44 | AI

What is the difference between pre-trained and fine-tuned models in generative AI ?

Answer

❖ Pre-trained models are trained on large datasets for general tasks (e.g. **GPT**, **BERT**).

❖ Fine-tuned models are adapted from pre-trained models for specific tasks using domain-specific data. Fine-tuning allows leveraging the general knowledge of pre-trained models while specializing them for targeted applications.

Question 45 | AI

What are the key differences between PyTorch's dynamic computation graph and TensorFlow's static graph ?

Answer

❖ **Dynamic Graph (PyTorch)** - Built at runtime, allowing flexibility and easier debugging.

❖ **Static Graph (TensorFlow)** - Defined before execution, enabling optimizations for production.

! Dynamic graphs are preferred for research, while static graphs are better for deployment.

Question 46 | AI

What are tokenization techniques in NLP ?

Answer

Tokenization splits text into smaller units (tokens) for processing.

- ❖ **Word-level tokenization** - Splits text into words.

- ❖ **Subword tokenization** (e.g. Byte Pair Encoding) - Breaks words into subword units, handling rare words better.

- ❖ **Character-level tokenization** - Splits text into individual characters.

Question 47 | AI

What is model drift ?

Answer

Model drift occurs when a model's performance degrades due to changes in data distribution over time.

Question 48 | AI

What are attention mechanisms in deep learning, and why are they important ?

Answer

Attention mechanisms allow models to focus on relevant parts of input data.

Self-attention (used in Transformers) - Computes relationships between all input tokens, enabling context-aware representations. Attention improves performance in tasks like machine translation, text summarization, and image captioning.

Question 49 | AI

What is the difference between batch inference and real-time inference in AI model deployment ?

Answer

❖ **Batch inference** - Processes multiple inputs at once, it is suitable for offline tasks (e.g. generating recommendations).

❖ **Real-time inference** - Processes single inputs instantly, it is suitable for interactive applications (e.g. chatbots). Batch inference is more efficient for large datasets, while real-time inference prioritizes low latency.

Question 50 | AI

How do you ensure reproducibility in AI experiments ?

Answer

❖ **Set random seeds** - Ensure consistent results by fixing random seeds for libraries like NumPy and PyTorch.

❖ **Version control** - Track code and dataset versions using tools like Git and DVC.

❖ **Environment management** - Use tools like Docker or Conda to replicate environments.

! Reproducibility is critical for validating AI research and ensuring consistent results.

Question 51 | AI

What is the difference between supervised and unsupervised learning ?

Answer

❖ **Supervised learning** - Models are trained on labeled data (e.g. classification, regression).

❖ **Unsupervised learning** - Models find patterns in unlabeled data (e.g. clustering, dimensionality reduction).

– **(ex) Supervised** - Predicting house prices based on features like size and location.

– **(ex) Unsupervised** - Grouping customers based on purchasing behavior.

Question 52 | AI

What are the main differences between discriminative and generative models in AI ?

Answer

❖ **Discriminative models** - Learn the boundary between classes (e.g. logistic regression, neural networks).

❖ **Generative models** - Learn the distribution of data to generate new samples (e.g. GANs, Variational Autoencoders).

Example

– A discriminative model predicts whether an email is spam or not.

– A generative model can create entirely new emails that resemble spam.

Question 53 | AI

How does reinforcement learning differ from supervised and unsupervised learning ?

Answer

Reinforcement learning (RL) trains agents through **reward-based feedback** instead of labeled data (supervised) or patterns (unsupervised).

❖ Agents interact with an environment and maximize cumulative rewards.

❖ Used in robotics, game-playing AI (e.g. AlphaGo), and autonomous systems.

Question 54 | AI

What are transformer models, and why have they revolutionized NLP ?

Answer

Transformers replace traditional sequential architectures like LSTMs by using **self-attention** for context-aware learning.

❖ They process entire input sequences in parallel instead of step-by-step.

❖ Models like BERT and GPT enable state-of-the-art results in NLP tasks like translation and sentiment analysis.

BERT understands word meaning based on context, unlike traditional bag-of-words models.

Question 55 | AI

What is zero-shot learning ?

Answer

Zero-shot learning enables AI models to **generalize** to tasks or categories they have never seen before.

❖ Used in NLP (e.g. GPT models answering questions without fine-tuning).

❖ Relies on **pre-existing knowledge** rather than labeled training data.

Example: A chatbot trained only on English conversation can answer basic questions in Spanish without explicit training.

Question 56 | AI

What are ethical concerns associated with AI-based decision-making systems ?

Answer

AI systems may reinforce biases or lack transparency in decision-making.

- ❖ Bias in hiring models can lead to discrimination.

- ❖ Credit-scoring models may favor certain demographics.

Solutions

- ✓ Audit models for fairness using fairness-aware algorithms.

- ✓ Ensure human oversight in AI-driven decisions.

Question 57 | AI

What is model explainability ?

Answer

Explainability helps users understand **how AI models make predictions**.

- ★ Important for trust in medical, financial, and legal applications.

Techniques

- ❖ Feature importance analysis.

- ❖ Visualization of decision boundaries.

- ❖ SHAP and LIME for explaining deep learning predictions.

Question 58 | AI

What are the key challenges in deploying AI models at scale, and how can they be addressed ?

Answer

Deploying AI models at scale presents challenges such as

- ❖ **Latency issues** - Real-time applications require fast inference.

- ❖ **Model drift** - Data distribution changes over time, degrading model performance.

- ❖ **Infrastructure scaling** - Handling millions of AI requests efficiently.

Solutions

- ✓ **Use optimized inference engines** like **TensorRT** or **ONNX Runtime**.
- ✓ **Implement model monitoring** to detect drift and retrain models periodically.
- ✓ **Scale infrastructure dynamically** with **Kubernetes** and cloud services (AWS, GCP, Azure).

Question 59 | AI

How do Python-based AI models ensure data privacy in

sensitive applications ?

Answer

Privacy-preserving techniques

Differential privacy: Introduces random noise to obscure individual data points.

Federated learning: Trains models across multiple devices without sharing raw data.

Homomorphic encryption: Allows AI computations on encrypted data without decryption.

These techniques help comply with GDPR and HIPAA regulations.

Question 60 | AI

What is differential privacy ?

Answer

Differential privacy introduces **controlled random noise** to training datasets, preventing individual user data from being exposed.

Advantages

❖ Protects user identity in sensitive applications.

❖ Ensures compliance with privacy laws (**GDPR, CCPA**).

❖ Enables AI models to learn **global trends** without storing personal data.

Question 61 | AI

How does AI optimize hyperparameter tuning, and what methods are commonly used ?

Answer

Hyperparameter tuning improves model performance by optimizing parameters that control training behavior.

Common methods

❖ **Grid Search** - Exhaustively evaluates predefined hyperparameter combinations.

❖ **Random Search** - Randomly selects hyperparameter values within a range.

❖ **Bayesian Optimization** - Estimates the best hyperparameters using probability models.

❖ **Neural Architecture Search (NAS)** - AI-driven optimization of deep learning architectures.

Hyperparameter tuning ensures AI models achieve optimal accuracy and generalization.

Question 62 | AI

What are AI-powered retrieval-augmented generation (RAG) models ?

Answer

RAG models combine information retrieval with generative models to provide more accurate responses.

- ❖ **Retrieval component** - Finds relevant external data based on user queries.

- ❖ **Generation component** - Uses deep learning (e.g. GPT) to formulate responses based on retrieved information.

Used in **question-answering systems**, **knowledge-grounded chatbots**, and **fact-checking AI**.

Question 63 | AI

What is multimodal AI ?

Answer

Multimodal AI processes multiple data types (e.g. text, images, audio) simultaneously.

❖ Improves **context-awareness** by integrating information across modalities.

❖ Used in **image-captioning systems, autonomous vehicles, and AI-powered diagnostics**.

Modern models like **CLIP** and **Gemini** leverage multimodal learning for **enhanced generalization**.

Question 64 | AI

What is AI-powered knowledge distillation ?

Answer

Knowledge distillation transfers knowledge from **large models to smaller, efficient models**.

Benefits

❖ Reduces **model size** while maintaining accuracy.

❖ Improves **deployment efficiency** on constrained devices.

❖ Enables **compressed AI models** for low-latency inference.

Used in **mobile AI applications, edge computing, and industrial automation**.

Question 65 | AI

What are adversarial AI attacks ?

Answer

Adversarial attacks manipulate **input data to deceive AI models** into incorrect predictions.

Examples

❖ **Pixel-level alterations** causing image misclassification.

❖ **AI-generated fraudulent text** bypassing spam filters.

Defensive Strategies

❖ **Adversarial training** exposing models to manipulated examples.

❖ **Robust loss functions** penalizing sensitive model behavior.

❖ **Input sanitization** filtering suspicious data before inference.

Question 66 | AI

What are edge AI applications, and how do they differ from cloud-based AI models ?

Answer

❖ **Edge AI -** Runs locally on devices (smartphones, IoT sensors) instead of relying on cloud computation.

❖ **Cloud AI -** Requires remote data processing in centralized servers.

Edge AI Advantages

❖ **Lower latency** (faster decision-making).

❖ **Reduced bandwidth consumption** by eliminating cloud transfers.

❖ **Better privacy** since data stays on local devices.

Used in autonomous vehicles, smart appliances, and medical diagnostics.

Question 67 | AI

How does the AI contribute to sustainable energy optimization ?

Answer

AI models analyze energy consumption patterns to

- ❖ Optimize smart grids, reducing electricity wastage.

- ❖ Enhance renewable energy forecasting, improving solar/wind efficiency.

- ❖ Reduce carbon emissions with AI-driven environmental monitoring.

AI-powered sustainability supports **eco-friendly innovations** and **climate-conscious industries**.

Question 68 | AI

What is AI model pruning ?

Answer

Pruning removes **redundant weights** from deep learning models, reducing computation.

Benefits

- ❖ **Lower memory usage**, ideal for mobile AI.

- ❖ **Faster inference speed** in time-critical applications.

- ❖ **Improved efficiency** without sacrificing accuracy.

Used in **AI-powered edge computing, IoT, and embedded AI devices**.

Question 69 | AI

How does AI-driven sentiment analysis improve customer experience ?

Answer

AI sentiment analysis **evaluates emotions from text, voice, and images**, improving user engagement.

Applications

- ❖ **AI-powered chatbots** adapt responses based on user tone.

- ❖ **Brand monitoring AI** detects customer sentiment shifts in social media.

- ❖ **Personalized advertising AI** tailors marketing strategies based on emotional trends.

Used in **customer support AI, e-commerce AI insights, and business intelligence platforms**.

Question 70 | AI

What are AI-powered digital twins ?

Answer

Digital twins **replicate real-world systems in AI-driven simulations**, enhancing analysis and optimization.

Benefits

- ❖ **Predictive modeling** for industrial equipment maintenance.

- ❖ **Real-time scenario testing** for urban planning and construction.

- ❖ **AI-enhanced prototyping** for medical, aerospace, and manufacturing sectors.

Used in **smart city development, AI-based engineering, and AI-assisted healthcare diagnostics**.

>>> Data Analysis

Question 71 | Data Analysis

What is the Data Wrangling in Pandas, and why is it important ?

Answer

Data wrangling is the process of **cleaning, transforming, and structuring raw data** into a format suitable for analysis. Pandas is a powerful Python library for data wrangling, enabling efficient manipulation of structured datasets.

The Main Operations in Pandas Data Wrangling

❖ Handling missing values (`fillna()`, `dropna()`).

❖ Merging and joining datasets (`merge()`, `concat()`).

❖ Transforming data formats (`pivot_table()`, `melt()`).

❖ Filtering and selecting specific rows/columns (`loc[]`, `iloc[]`).

Data wrangling ensures **data integrity**, making it usable for machine learning models or business decisions.

Question 72 | Data Analysis

What is the difference between .loc[] and .iloc[] in Pandas ?

Answer

❖ .loc[] selects data using **labels** (row/column names).
❖ .iloc[] selects data using **integer positions** (row/column index).

Example Code

```
import pandas as pd

df = pd.DataFrame({"A": [10, 20, 30], "B":
                  [40, 50, 60]}, index=["x", "y", "z"])

print(df.loc["x"])   # Selects row by label
print(df.iloc[0])    # Selects row by position
```

.loc[] is ideal when working with **named indices**, while .iloc[] is preferred for **numeric indexing**.

Question 73 | Data Analysis

How does the NumPy improve numerical computing efficiency ?

Answer

NumPy provides **fast, optimized array operations**, making it far superior to Python lists for numerical computing.

Advantages

❖ **Vectorized operations** (`np.add()`, `np.multiply()`), eliminating slow loops.

❖ **Memory efficiency**, as NumPy arrays consume **less memory** than lists.

❖ **Built-in mathematical functions** (`np.sqrt()`, `np.log()`), optimizing performance.

❖ **Broadcasting**, enabling element-wise operations on mismatched array shapes.

NumPy is essential for **scientific computing, machine learning, and large-scale numerical processing**.

Question 74 | Data Analysis

What is broadcasting in NumPy, and how does it work ?

Answer

Broadcasting enables NumPy operations on arrays **of different shapes** without explicit looping.

Example Code

```
import numpy as np

a = np.array([1, 2, 3])
```

```
b = np.array([[10], [20], [30]]) # Different shape but ok
result = a + b  # Broadcasting happens here
```

Instead of iterating, NumPy **expands dimensions intelligently** to perform element-wise operations efficiently.

Question 75 | Data Analysis

How does Streamlit simplify interactive dashboard development ?

Answer

Streamlit allows Python devs to build interactive web dashboards without complex frontend coding.

Features

❖ **Quick setup** - No HTML/CSS required, uses simple Python scripts.

❖ **Widgets** - Interactive elements (`st.slider()`, `st.selectbox()`).

❖ **Data visualization integration** - Supports **Matplotlib**, **Seaborn**, **Plotly**.

Question 76 | Data Analysis

How does Streamlit simplify interactive dashboard development ?

Answer

Each visualization library has its strengths

Library	Best Use Case
Matplotlib	Custom plots, static charts
Seaborn	Statistical visualizations, default styling
Plotly	Interactive, web-friendly charts

Plotly is interactive, while Matplotlib is highly customizable, and Seaborn is optimized for data analysis.

Question 77 | Data Analysis

How do you visualize time-series data with Matplotlib ?

Answer

Time-series plots track trends over time, major for forecasting.

Example Code

```
import matplotlib.pyplot as plt
import pandas as pd

data = pd.Series([10, 20, 30, 25],
index=pd.date_range("2023-01-01", periods=4))
data.plot(marker="o")
plt.title("Time-Series Plot")
plt.show()
```

Result

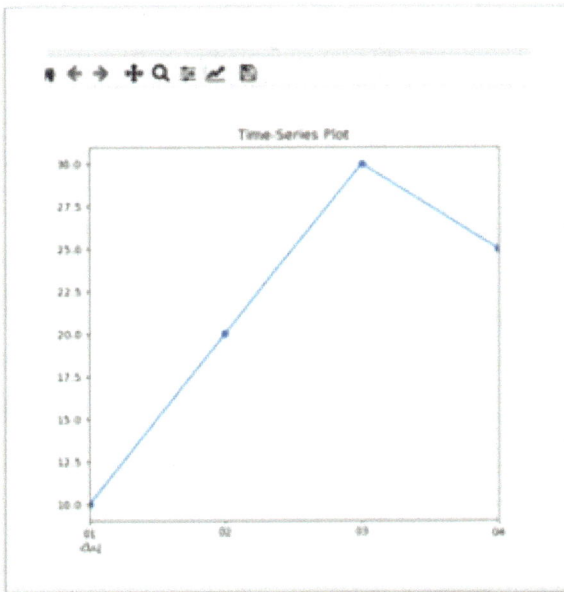

Used in finance, sales forecasting, and performance tracking.

Question 78 | Data Analysis

How do you create interactive bar charts with Plotly ?

Answer

Plotly enables dynamic, hover-friendly visualizations.

Example Code

```
import plotly.express as px

df = px.data.gapminder()
fig = px.bar(df[df["year"] == 2007], x="country",
y="gdpPercap", color="continent")
fig.show()
```

This makes Plotly ideal for real-time dashboards and web applications.

Example output:

Question 79 | Data Analysis

What are some common statistical functions in NumPy ?

Answer

np.mean()	Computes the mean
np.median()	Finds the median
np.std()	Calculates standard deviation
np.var()	Computes variance

These functions help summarize datasets efficiently.

Question 80 | Data Analysis

How does NumPy handle broadcasting ?

Answer

Broadcasting allows **automatic expansion of smaller arrays** when performing operations with larger ones.

Example Code

```
import numpy as np

arr1 = np.array([1, 2, 3])
arr2 = np.array([[10], [20], [30]])

result = arr1 + arr2 # Broadcasting expands arr2
```

It eliminates the need for explicit loops, making computations more efficient.

Question 81 | Data Analysis

How does Streamlit improve interactive visualization compared to Jupyter Notebooks ?

Answer

❖ **Web-friendly** - Generates fully interactive web applications.

❖ **Better interactivity** - Supports sliders, buttons, and real-time updates.

❖ **Simplifies deployment** - Can be hosted online without complex setup.

Question 82 | Data Analysis

How do you create a grouped bar chart using Matplotlib ?

Answer

```
import matplotlib.pyplot as plt
import numpy as np

categories = ["A", "B", "C"]
values1 = [10, 20, 30]
values2 = [15, 25, 35]

x = np.arange(len(categories))
width = 0.4   # Bar width

plt.bar(x, values1, width, label="Group 1")
plt.bar(x + width, values2, width, label="Group 2")
plt.xticks(x + width / 2, categories)
plt.legend()
plt.show()
```

Grouped bar charts compare values across multiple categories.

Example output image:

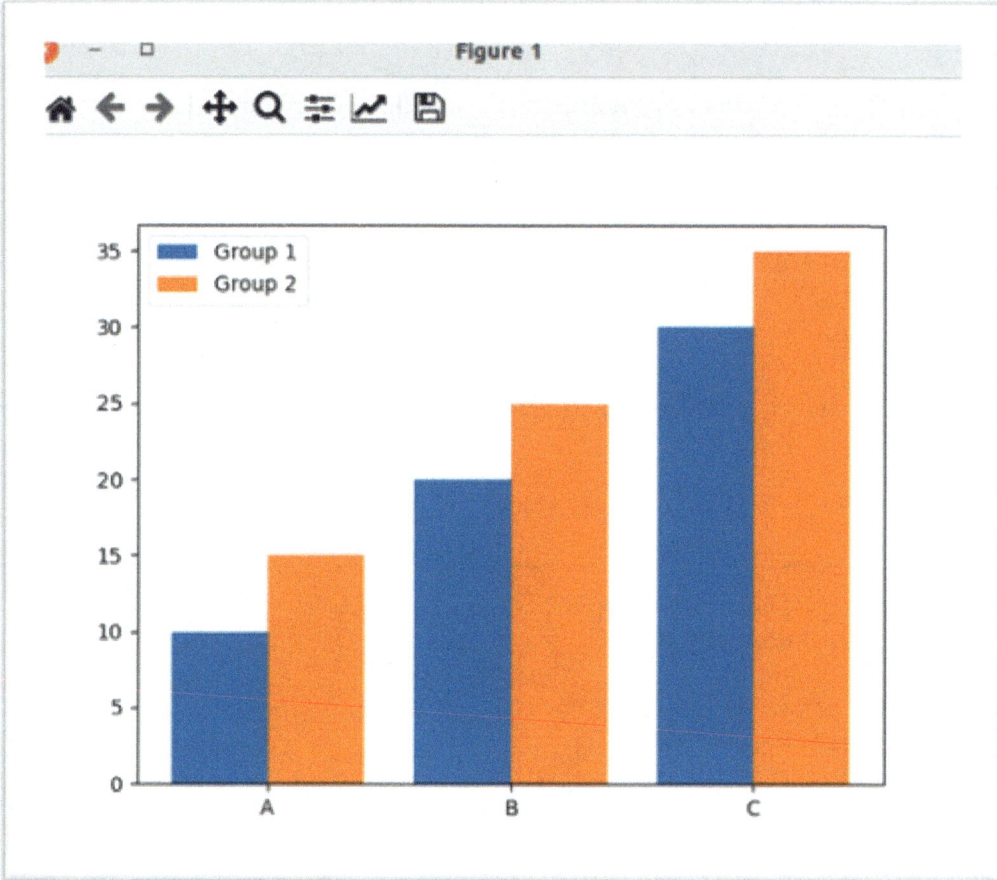

Question 83 | Data Analysis

How do you optimize the large-scale data operations in Pandas ?

Answer

Large datasets can slow Pandas operations due to high memory usage and inefficient computations.

Optimizing data processing

- ✓ **Using vectorized operations** (`df.apply()` instead of loops).
- ✓ **Reducing memory footprint** (`astype()` to convert data types).
- ✓ **Lazy loading** using dask for parallel computing.
- ✓ **Filtering data early** to minimize processed rows.

Question 84 | Data Analysis

How does NumPy enable faster matrix operations compared to native Python lists ?

Answer

NumPy is optimized for numerical computing due to

- ❖ Contiguous memory storage, reducing overhead.
- ❖ Vectorized execution, eliminating Python loops.

❖ Built-in mathematical functions, preventing redundant operations.

Example Code

```python
import numpy as np

a = np.array([1, 2, 3])
b = np.array([4, 5, 6])
result = np.dot(a, b)   # Fast dot product computation
```

NumPy is essential for **linear algebra, AI model optimization, and large-scale numerical simulations**.

Question 85 | Data Analysis

How does `.merge()` differ from `.join()` in Pandas ?

Answer

Both .merge() and .join() combine datasets, but they differ in their approach.

❖ `.merge()` is used for SQL-style joins, requiring explicit on column specification.

❖ `.join()` works on index-based merges, simplifying integration of related datasets.

Useful in **database integration, data warehousing, and relational data processing**.

Question 86 | Data Analysis

What is .astype() in Pandas, and how does it optimize data processing ?

Answer

`.astype()` converts data types to reduce memory usage and improve performance. Used in large-scale analytics and big data processing.

Question 87 | Data Analysis

How does NumPy's einsum() improve performance over standard matrix multiplication ?

Answer

`einsum()` is a highly efficient function for tensor contractions, avoiding unnecessary data movement.

- ❖ Optimizes multi-dimensional operations, reducing memory usage.
- ❖ Faster than standard loops and `np.dot()` in specific cases.

Example Code

```
import numpy as np

A = np.random.rand(100, 100)
B = np.random.rand(100, 100)
```

```
result = np.einsum("ij,jk->ik", A, B)
# Matrix Mult via Einstein summation
```

Used in **quantum computing, AI model optimizations, and high-performance numerical simulations**.

Question 88 | Data Analysis

What is the difference between st.table() and st.dataframe() in Streamlit ?

Answer

❖ st.table() - This function is used for displaying static tables. It renders the table as a simple, uneditable HTML table and is best suited for presenting small datasets that do not require interactivity. The formatting is fixed, and users cannot sort, filter, or interact with the table.

❖ st.dataframe() - This function provides an interactive table using Pandas' DataFrame. It allows users to sort columns, scroll through large datasets, and even modify the data (if supported). It's ideal for handling larger datasets where interactivity is useful.

If you need a simple, formatted table for display purposes, st.table() is the way to go. If you want users to interact with the data dynamically, st.dataframe() is more powerful.

Question 89 | Data Analysis

What are the differences between `.hist()` and `sns.kdeplot()` for data distribution visualization ?

Answer

- ❖ `.hist()` shows discrete frequency distributions.
- ❖ `sns.kdeplot()` smooths distributions with a kernel density function.

Used in risk analysis and behavioral data insights.

Question 90 | Data Analysis

How do you optimize Pandas operations for handling large datasets ?

Answer

Handling large datasets efficiently in Pandas requires **reducing memory usage, optimizing operations, and leveraging parallel computing**.

- ❖ **Reduce memory footprint**: Convert columns to appropriate data types (e.g. categorical variables instead of strings).

- ❖ **Use vectorized operations**: Avoid Python loops and apply built-in Pandas functions (`applymap()`, `agg()`).

- ❖ **Filter data early**: Load only necessary columns and rows using query-based filtering.

❖ **Leverage Dask for parallel computing**: Instead of Pandas, Dask enables distributed processing of large datasets without exhausting RAM.

These optimizations are crucial for **big data analytics, machine learning preprocessing, and financial modeling**.

>>> Advanced Python

Question 91 | Advanced Python

What are type hints in Python, and how do they improve code reliability ?

Answer

Type hints allow devs to specify **expected data types** for function arguments and return values, improving code clarity and reducing runtime errors.

Benefits

❖ Enhances code readability, helping developers understand function behavior.

❖ Allows static type checking using tools like MyPy to detect type inconsistencies before execution.

❖ Improves IDE support, providing intelligent auto-completion and debugging assistance.

Python type hints do not enforce strict typing at runtime, but they guide linters and static analysis tools for better code quality.

Question 92 | Advanced Python

How do you create a custom decorator ?

Answer

```python
def my_decorator(func):
    def wrapper(*args, **kwargs):
        print("Executing function...")
        result = func(*args, **kwargs)
        print("Execution complete.")
        return result
    return wrapper

@my_decorator
def say_hello():
    print("Hello, World!")
```

In this example, my_decorator modifies say_hello() by adding pre-processing and post-processing logic.

Question 93 | Advanced Python

What is the difference between function decorators and class decorators ?

Answer

❖ Function decorators modify the behavior of functions or methods.

❖ Class decorators modify the behavior of entire classes, typically altering attribute initialization or method execution.

Use Cases

❖ Function decorators handle logging, authorization, memoization.

❖ Class decorators assist with automatic property validation, singleton patterns, and dynamic attribute modification.

Question 94 | Advanced Python

How do context managers in Python help manage resources effectively ?

Answer

Context managers automate resource management using with statements, ensuring proper allocation and cleanup (like closing files or releasing locks).

Advantages

❖ Prevents resource leaks by ensuring cleanup after usage.
❖ Improves code readability by abstracting manual cleanup.
❖ Reduces error handling complexity, providing a structured approach to resource control.

Common use cases include **file handling, database connections, network requests, and thread synchronization**.

Question 95 | Advanced Python

How do you implement a custom context manager ?

Answer

```python
class MyResource:
    def __enter__(self):
        print("Resource acquired")
        return self

    def __exit__(self, exc_type, exc_value, traceback):
        print("Resource released")

with MyResource():
    print("Using resource")
```

This ensures __exit__() is always executed, preventing resource leaks.

Question 96 | Advanced Python

How do metaclasses work, and when should you use them ?

Answer

A metaclass controls class creation, allowing automatic method injections, validation, or transformations.

❖ Metaclasses inherit from type and override __new__() or __init__() to modify behavior.

❖ Used in ORM frameworks, API validation, and automatic property generation.

Metaprogramming is powerful but complex, recommended for framework developers and advanced Python engineers.

Question 97 | Advanced Python

What is static type checking ?

Answer

MyPy performs static type checking, ensuring consistency without enforcing strict typing at runtime.

❖ Detects type mismatches before execution.
❖ Improves IDE autocompletion and documentation accuracy.
❖ Reduces runtime errors by validating function signatures.

Used in enterprise applications, collaborative projects, and large-scale codebases.

Question 98 | Advanced Python

What are the benefits of using `functools.wraps()` in Python decorators ?

Answer

- ❖ Preserves original function metadata (name, docstring, annotations).
- ❖ Prevents unintended behavior in decorated functions.
- ❖ Improves debugging by retaining original attributes instead of wrapper references.

Essential for ensuring decorated functions maintain their expected properties.

Question 99 | Advanced Python

How do Python's `@staticmethod` and `@classmethod` decorators differ ?

Answer

- ❖ `@staticmethod` does not access instance or class attributes, behaving like a normal function within a class.

- ❖ `@classmethod` receives the class itself (`cls`) as an argument, allowing modification at the class level.

Use `@staticmethod` for **utility functions**, and `@classmethod` for **factory methods**.

Question 100 | Advanced Python

What are the benefits of using static typing in Python, and how does MyPy assist with type checking ?

Answer

Static typing improves code reliability, readability, and maintainability by allowing developers to define expected data types. MyPy helps by performing static analysis, detecting type errors before runtime, and preventing unexpected failures. Static typing also enables better IDE support and code completion, making large-scale applications easier to manage.

Question 101 | Advanced Python

How does Python's typing system handle optional types ?

Answer

Optional types are handled using Optional[T], indicating that a variable can either be of type T or None. This is crucial for functions that may or may not return values, ensuring better type safety and reducing ambiguity in function outputs. Without explicitly specifying optional types, unexpected NoneType errors might occur during execution.

Question 102 | Advanced Python

What are common use cases for function decorators ?

Answer

❖ **Logging decorator**: Tracks execution times and function calls for debugging.

❖ **Memoization decorator**: Caches function results to avoid redundant computations.

❖ **Authentication decorator**: Validates user permissions before function execution.

❖ **Rate-limiting decorator**: Prevents excessive API calls by enforcing limits.

Each decorator helps enhance functionality while keeping core business logic separate.

Question 103 | Advanced Python

What are the differences between manual resource management and context managers ?

Answer

Manual resource management requires explicit cleanup, increasing the risk of leaks if exceptions occur before resource release. Context managers using with statements automate resource allocation and deallocation, ensuring safe cleanup, reducing bugs, and improving readability in operations like file handling, database connections, and network requests.

Question 104 | Advanced Python

What are metaclasses ?

Answer

Metaclasses define class behavior, enabling automatic modifications at the creation stage. They are useful for enforcing coding standards, injecting dynamic methods, creating singleton patterns, and implementing ORM frameworks. Since metaprogramming adds complexity, it should be used only when dynamic class transformations are necessary.

Question 105 | Advanced Python

What are abstract base classes (ABCs) ?

Answer

ABCs define blueprints for child classes without implementing full functionality. They enforce required methods and attributes, ensuring subclasses meet expected contracts. Python's abc module enables structured design in large applications, improving extensibility in plugin architectures, ORM frameworks, and API standardization.

Question 106 | Advanced Python

How does introspection help in debugging and metaprogramming ?

Answer

Introspection allows examining Python objects at runtime, providing valuable insights into attributes, methods, and types.

It helps dynamically

- ❖ Retrieve method lists (`dir()`).
- ❖ Inspect function signatures (`inspect.signature()`).
- ❖ Modify class attributes (`setattr()`, `getattr()`).

Introspection is vital for debugging, API validation, and dynamic function generation.

Question 107 | Advanced Python

What are covariance and contravariance in Python's type hints ?

Answer

Covariance and contravariance define type relationships for function arguments and return types in generic type hints.

❖ Covariant types allow subtype substitution for return values.

❖ Contravariant types allow subtype substitution for function parameters.

Understanding these concepts enhances type safety in generic programming and API design.

Question 108 | Advanced Python

Why should you avoid using mutable default arguments in functions ?

Answer

Using mutable defaults like lists or dictionaries leads to unexpected state retention across multiple function calls.

❖ The default mutable object is shared between function calls, leading to unintended modifications.

❖ Instead, use None as the default and initialize inside the function to prevent persistent mutation.

This issue is a common pitfall and must be handled carefully in API and function design.

Question 109 | Advanced Python

How does decorator chaining work, and what are common use cases ?

Answer

Decorator chaining applies multiple decorators to a function, modifying its behavior step by step.

❖ The execution order follows bottom-up, meaning the innermost decorator executes first.

❖ Common use cases include authentication checks, logging, caching, and access control mechanisms.

Understanding decorator chaining helps structure reusable code patterns efficiently.

Question 110 | Advanced Python

How do descriptor objects enhance class attribute management ?

Answer

Descriptors provide custom behavior for attribute access, modification, and deletion via __get__(), __set__(), and __delete__().

❖ Used for computed properties, lazy attribute evaluation, and validation mechanisms.

❖ The property built-in decorator is a common example of a descriptor.

Descriptors help enforce strict control over class attributes, improving encapsulation.

Question 111 | Advanced Python

What are weak references, and how do they help manage memory ?

Answer

Weak references allow referencing objects without preventing garbage collection.

❖ Used in caching systems, circular reference handling, and memory-efficient lookups.

❖ Available via the weakref module, ensuring objects get removed when no longer needed.

Weak references help optimize memory usage in long-running applications.

Question 112 | Advanced Python

How does Python handle monkey patching, and when should it be avoided ?

Answer

Monkey patching dynamically modifies objects or modules at runtime.

- ❖ Used in hotfixes, debugging, and extending third-party libraries.

- ❖ However, it reduces maintainability and creates unpredictable dependencies, so use with caution.

It is recommended to use dependency injection or subclassing instead of direct modification.

Question 113 | Advanced Python

How does Python's method resolution order (MRO) affect class inheritance ?

Answer

MRO defines the order in which classes are searched for methods, ensuring predictable execution.

- ❖ Python follows C3 linearization, creating a consistent method lookup chain.

❖ MRO avoids conflicts in multiple inheritance scenarios, making diamond structures manageable.

Understanding MRO is essential for designing complex multi-class architectures.

Question 114 | Advanced Python

What is the difference between runtime type checking and static type checking ?

Answer

❖ **Runtime type checking** occurs during execution, where Python dynamically determines variable types. Errors are detected only when the code runs.

❖ **Static type checking** ensures type correctness before execution using tools like MyPy. It prevents common mistakes like passing an unexpected type without running the code.

Question 115 | Advanced Python

Why __slots__ improve performance ?

Answer

__slots__ restricts object attributes, preventing dynamic dictionary overhead.

❖ Reduces memory footprint in high-volume object creation.
❖ Improves lookup speed in performance-critical applications.

Question 116 | Advanced Python

Why should you use __slots__ in Python classes ?

Answer

Using __slots__ in Python classes optimizes memory by preventing the creation of a dynamic __dict__, restricting attributes to a predefined set, leading to faster access and reduced overhead, making it beneficial for large-scale object instances but limiting flexibility in dynamic attribute assignment.

Example Code

```
class OptimizedClass:
    __slots__ = ("name", "age")

p = OptimizedClass()
p.name = "Alice" # Works
# p.address = "Unknown"  # Raises an AttributeError!
```

Used in large-scale AI models, memory-optimized applications, and high-performance data processing.

>>> Asynchronous Programming and Real-Time Systems

Question 117 | Async Programming and RTS

What is an event loop in Python's asyncio, and why is it important ?

Answer

An event loop is the core component of asynchronous execution in Python. It manages and schedules asynchronous tasks, ensuring they run efficiently without blocking the main execution thread.

❖ It continuously monitors coroutines and I/O operations, executing them when resources are available.

❖ The loop enables concurrent execution in a single-threaded environment, preventing the need for explicit multithreading.

Example Code

```python
import asyncio

async def main():
    print("Hello, Async!")
    await asyncio.sleep(1)
    print("Goodbye, Async!")
```

```
asyncio.run(main()) # Starts the event loop
```

Question 118 | Async Programming and RTS

What is the difference between `asyncio.gather()` and `asyncio.create_task()` ?

Answer

❖ `asyncio.gather()` collects multiple coroutines and executes them together, ensuring results are returned as a list.

❖ `asyncio.create_task()` schedules coroutines independently, allowing execution in the background.

`create_task()` is ideal for fire-and-forget operations, while `gather()` is best for handling multiple dependent tasks.

Question 119 | Async Programming and RTS

What is await ?

Answer

await pauses function execution until an async task completes, preventing blocking and allowing other coroutines to run.

❖ Used to wait for asynchronous responses.
❖ Ensures functions execute non-blocking operations efficiently.

Question 120 | Async Programming and RTS

How does `aiohttp` improve HTTP requests in asynchronous applications ?

Answer

aiohttp is an asynchronous HTTP client and server library, allowing non-blocking network interactions.

- ❖ Unlike requests, aiohttp enables parallel execution using asyncio.

- ❖ Supports WebSockets, asynchronous streaming, and connection pooling.

- ❖ Ideal for high-performance APIs, microservices, and large-scale crawlers.

It reduces latency in network-intensive applications.

Question 121 | Async Programming and RTS

What are WebSockets, and how do they enable real-time communication ?

Answer

WebSockets provide full-duplex, bidirectional communication between clients and servers.

❖ Unlike traditional HTTP, WebSockets maintain persistent connections, reducing latency.

❖ Used in chat applications, real-time dashboards, stock market data feeds, and multiplayer gaming.

❖ Supports binary and text-based messages, enabling flexible data exchange.

WebSockets are fundamental to high-performance interactive applications.

Question 122 | Async Programming and RTS

How does Trio simplify asynchronous programming compared to asyncio ?

Answer

Trio is a structured concurrency framework that simplifies async workflows.

❖ Eliminates callback nesting, making code easier to read than traditional asyncio.
❖ Supports safe cancellation, reducing race conditions.
❖ Provides automatic error propagation, preventing silent failures.

Trio is preferred for more maintainable async code in production applications.

Question 123 | Async Programming and RTS

What are the key differences between traditional threading and async programming ?

Answer

Feature	Async (asyncio)	Threading (threading)
Execution Model	Event-driven	Preemptive scheduling
Ideal Use Case	I/O-bound tasks	CPU-bound tasks
Memory Consumption	Low	Higher due to threads
Blocking Behavior	Non-blocking	May cause race conditions

Threading is better for parallel computations, while async programming excels in I/O-driven workflows.

Question 124 | Async Programming and RTS

What are structured concurrency principles, and how does Trio implement them ?

Answer

Structured concurrency ensures that all async tasks are properly tracked, completed, or canceled, avoiding orphaned coroutines.

- ❖ Trio enforces structured concurrency by ensuring tasks exit cleanly.
- ❖ Prevents race conditions and memory leaks common in traditional async implementations.
- ❖ Uses nurseries (`trio.open_nursery()`) to create isolated execution groups for async tasks.

Structured concurrency prevents silent failures and improves reliability in production async code.

Question 125 | Async Programming and RTS

What are cancellation tokens in asyncio, and how do they help manage async workflows ?

Answer

Cancellation tokens allow safe termination of async tasks before completion.

- ❖ Used in timeouts, shutdown sequences, and controlled exits.

- ❖ Prevents tasks from running beyond required conditions, improving responsiveness.

- ❖ Ensures graceful cleanup without corrupting shared resources.

Canceling a coroutine avoids wasted computation and optimizes system performance.

Question 126 | Async Programming and RTS

How does `asyncio.Semaphore` prevent resource overuse in concurrent async tasks ?

Answer

A semaphore controls the number of concurrent executions, preventing overload on external systems like APIs and databases.

- ❖ Limits access to shared resources in an async event loop.
- ❖ Prevents excessive parallel requests, improving stability.
- ❖ Used in rate-limiting API calls and database connections.

Example scenario

- ❖ Setting a max semaphore count prevents excessive concurrent API requests, ensuring server reliability.

Question 127 | Async Programming and RTS

How do message queues enhance communication between asynchronous components ?

Answer

Message queues enable decoupled data exchange, improving modularity and scalability in async applications.

- ❖ Helps with producer-consumer workflows, preventing blocking.

❖ Supports distributed processing, where multiple consumers handle data asynchronously.

❖ Reduces latency in high-traffic data pipelines.

Common async queues include RabbitMQ, Kafka, and `asyncio.Queue()`.

Question 128 | Async Programming and RTS

How do asyncio signals (`loop.add_signal_handler()`) improve real-time systems ?

Answer

Signals allow the event loop to respond dynamically to system interrupts, improving async task management.

❖ Used to gracefully shut down applications on SIGINT or SIGTERM.

❖ Ensures ongoing async tasks complete before process termination.

❖ Critical for server applications needing controlled shutdown mechanisms.

Question 129 | Async Programming and RTS

How do backpressure handling techniques improve real-time streaming applications ?

Answer

Backpressure occurs when data producers overwhelm consumers, leading to lag or memory overflow.

- ❖ Apply rate limits (`asyncio.Semaphore`) to slow down producers.
- ❖ Use bounded queues (`asyncio.Queue(maxsize)`) to regulate data flow.
- ❖ Drop excess data when queues are full, ensuring smooth operation.

Backpressure handling is key to high-performance async streaming applications.

Question 130 | Async Programming and RTS

How does Python's async IO model handle thousands of concurrent connections efficiently ?

Answer

Python's async I/O model relies on event-driven execution, preventing blocking by scheduling tasks when resources are available.

- ❖ Uses epoll or kqueue, ensuring high-performance I/O event handling without spawning excessive threads.

❖ Efficiently manages network sockets, API calls, and WebSockets without thread pool overhead.

❖ Supports frameworks like aiohttp that optimize HTTP client-server interaction for high-volume requests.

The async I/O model enables scalable network communication while minimizing resource usage.

Question 131 | Async Programming and RTS

What are async lifecycle hooks, and why are they important in real-time systems ?

Answer

Async lifecycle hooks allow automatic execution at specific stages of coroutine lifecycles.

❖ Helps initialize resources, ensuring clean setup before processing.
❖ Provides shutdown sequences, allowing controlled resource cleanup.
❖ Used in event-driven frameworks to trigger callbacks dynamically.

Lifecycle hooks improve stability and fault tolerance in async-driven applications.

Question 132 | Async Programming and RTS

Why does Python recommend using bounded async queues for high-performance systems ?

Answer

Bounded queues (`asyncio.Queue(maxsize)`) prevent unlimited buffer growth, ensuring predictable memory usage.

- ❖ Protects against system overload in streaming applications.
- ❖ Ensures controlled data flow, optimizing real-time processing.
- ❖ Reduces memory consumption in high-frequency event-driven workflows.

Bounded queues are essential for high-throughput async architectures.

Question 133 | Async Programming and RTS

What are async watchdog timers, and how do they improve system reliability ?

Answer

Watchdog timers monitor coroutine execution time, preventing endless stalls.

- ❖ Terminates unresponsive tasks, ensuring system remains operational.

❖ Used in network monitoring, API timeouts, and real-time failure detection.

❖ Improves fault-tolerance in long-running async applications.

Watchdog timers enhance stability by preventing frozen async operations.

>>> Concurrency and Parallelism

Question 134 | Concurrency and Parallelism

What is difference between concurrency and parallelism ?

Answer

- ❖ Concurrency allows multiple tasks to make progress without necessarily executing simultaneously. Tasks switch execution rapidly but may share a single CPU core.

- ❖ Parallelism ensures multiple tasks run simultaneously, using multiple CPU cores or separate machines.

In Python

- ❖ Threads enable concurrency, but due to the Global Interpreter Lock (GIL), they do not achieve parallelism.

- ❖ Multiprocessing and distributed computing enable true parallelism by running processes independently.

Concurrency helps improve responsiveness, while parallelism maximizes compute efficiency across multiple resources.

Question 135 | Concurrency and Parallelism

How does the Global Interpreter Lock (GIL) affect multithreading ?

Answer

The GIL prevents multiple threads from executing Python bytecode simultaneously, limiting true parallel execution.

❖ It ensures thread safety but reduces multithreading efficiency for CPU-bound tasks.

❖ I/O-bound tasks benefit from threading since the GIL releases control during blocking I/O operations.

To bypass GIL constraints, use:

❖ Multiprocessing (multiprocessing module) for CPU-bound workloads.

❖ Async programming (asyncio) for I/O-bound tasks.

❖ External libraries like NumPy, which release the GIL for specific operations.

Understanding the GIL helps optimize task execution strategies effectively.

Question 136 | Concurrency and Parallelism

What are the differences between threads, processes, and async tasks ?

Answer

Feature	Threads	Processes	Async (asyncio)
Execution Model	Concurrent	Parallel	Cooperative multitasking
Use Case	I/O-bound	CPU-bound	I/O-bound
Resource Sharing	Shared memory	Separate memory space	Event-driven execution
Limitations	Affected by GIL	Higher memory overhead	Requires async-aware APIs

Question 137 | Concurrency and Parallelism

How does multiprocessing overcome the limitations of the GIL ?

Answer

❖ Multiprocessing creates separate processes, each with its own Python interpreter and memory space.

❖ Since each process runs independently, they bypass the GIL and achieve true parallel execution on multiple CPU cores.

❖ Best suited for CPU-heavy tasks like image processing, data compression, and scientific computation.

❖ Process-based execution is heavier than threading, as processes do not share memory directly.

Multiprocessing enables scalable workloads while avoiding GIL bottlenecks.

Question 138 | Concurrency and Parallelism

What are the advantages of using Dask for parallel computing ?

Answer

Dask is a parallel computing framework that scales Python code effortlessly.

❖ Supports large datasets that do not fit into memory.

❖ Uses lazy evaluation, breaking down tasks dynamically for distributed execution.

❖ Integrates with NumPy and Pandas, allowing parallel dataframe processing.

❖ Works across multi-core CPUs and distributed clusters, offering flexibility for parallel workloads.

Dask is ideal for big data processing, enabling parallel execution on large datasets.

Question 139 | Concurrency and Parallelism

How does Ray improve distributed parallel computing compared to traditional multiprocessing ?

Answer

Ray provides a fault-tolerant, distributed execution framework for scaling applications.

❖ Optimized for machine learning, reinforcement learning, and distributed computing.

❖ Uses actor-based parallelism, allowing stateful tasks across multiple nodes.

❖ Supports dynamic scaling, meaning workers can be added or removed based on workload demand.

Ray enhances Python's scalability by enabling parallel execution across multiple machines.

Question 140 | Concurrency and Parallelism

What is the difference between thread pools and process pools ?

Answer

❖ Thread pools (`concurrent.futures.ThreadPoolExecutor`) execute multiple threads within the same process, suitable for I/O-bound operations.

❖ Process pools (`concurrent.futures.ProcessPoolExecutor`) spawn multiple processes, ideal for CPU-heavy tasks that need parallel execution.

❖ Processes run separately, bypassing the GIL, while threads share memory but must obey GIL constraints.

Choosing the right pool type optimizes concurrency for different workloads.

Question 141 | Concurrency and Parallelism

How does Python support distributed parallel execution with Ray actors ?

Answer

Ray enables parallel execution of stateful tasks using actors.

❖ Actors persist across multiple function calls, unlike traditional function-based execution.

❖ Allows dynamic workload distribution, improving real-time scaling.

❖ Used for AI model serving, reinforcement learning, and parallel task execution across clusters.

Actors enhance fault tolerance and scalability in large parallel systems.

Question 142 | Concurrency and Parallelism

Why is it important to use `multiprocessing.Queue()` instead of `queue.Queue()` in parallel processes ?

Answer

❖ `queue.Queue()` works only within threads, requiring shared memory access.

❖ `multiprocessing.Queue()` enables inter-process communication, supporting parallel execution across multiple CPU cores.

❖ Ensures safe exchange of data, avoiding GIL-related constraints.

Using the appropriate queue enhances performance in parallel execution models.

Question 143 | Concurrency and Parallelism

What are lock-free data structures, and how do they improve parallel computing ?

Answer

Lock-free data structures eliminate the need for explicit locking, preventing thread contention.

❖ Reduces synchronization overhead, ensuring faster execution.

❖ Used for real-time concurrent queues, parallel sort algorithms, and atomic variables.

❖ Common in high-frequency trading systems and optimized database transactions.

Lock-free structures ensure efficient parallelism without manual synchronization.

Question 144 | Concurrency and Parallelism

What are the key differences between Python's asyncio and multi-threading for concurrency ?

Answer

Feature	asyncio	Threading
Execution Model	Cooperative multitasking	Preemptive scheduling
Use Case	I/O-bound tasks	I/O-bound tasks (GIL limited)

Blocking Behavior	Non-blocking	May block due to GIL
Memory Consumption	Lower	Higher due to threading overhead

Async is ideal for I/O-heavy applications, while threading is better for background tasks requiring concurrency.

Question 145 | Concurrency and Parallelism

What are real-world applications of parallel computing in Python ?

Answer

❖ **Machine Learning Training**: Distributed training across GPUs using Ray.

❖ **Big Data Processing**: Parallel dataframe computations with Dask.

❖ **Financial Modeling**: Multi-threaded high-frequency trading algorithms.

❖ **Scientific Simulations**: Physics and climate modeling on supercomputers.

Question 146 | Concurrency and Parallelism

What are Ray tasks, and how do they enable parallel execution ?

Answer

Ray provides fault-tolerant parallel computing, ideal for machine learning workflows.

- ❖ Enables distributed task execution using lightweight parallelization.
- ❖ Supports dynamic scaling, meaning workers adapt to workload demands.

Example Code

```
import ray

ray.init()

@ray.remote
def cpt(n):
    return n ** 2

# Distributed execution
results = ray.get([cpt.remote(i) for i in range(10)])
print(results)
```

Ray improves scalability across clusters for parallel processing.

Question 147 | Concurrency and Parallelism

How does Python handle inter-process communication (IPC) in parallel computing ?

Answer

Python provides several IPC mechanisms to exchange data between multiple processes.

❖ **Multiprocessing Pipes** (`multiprocessing.Pipe()`) for bidirectional data transfer.

❖ **Shared memory** (`multiprocessing.shared_memory`) for efficient large dataset processing.

❖ **Queues** (`multiprocessing.Queue()`) for producer-consumer communication.

❖ **Sockets** (`socket`) for networked distributed systems.

Question 148 | Concurrency and Parallelism

What is False Sharing ?

Answer

False sharing is a performance degradation issue that occurs in multi-threaded applications when multiple threads modify variables that reside in the same cache line, leading to unnecessary cache invalidation and memory contention. This phenomenon can significantly reduce the efficiency of concurrent applications, especially those running on multi-core processors.

Processors use cache memory to store frequently accessed data, reducing the need for slower memory (RAM) accesses. The cache is divided into cache lines, typically ranging from 32 to 128 bytes in size. When multiple variables share the same cache line and different threads modify these variables concurrently, performance suffers due to frequent cache invalidations.

Question 149 | Concurrency and Parallelism

How does cache line size affect false sharing in multi-threading ?

Answer

❖ Most modern processors have cache lines ranging from 32 to 128 bytes.

❖ If multiple threads modify variables that fall within the same cache line, each update forces the cache line to be invalidated and reloaded.

❖ This leads to increased memory bus traffic, reducing execution efficiency.

❖ The larger the cache line size, the greater the chance of false sharing when variables are packed closely in memory.

Question 150 | Concurrency and Parallelism

What is cache thrashing in multi-threaded applications, and how does it affect performance ?

Answer

Cache thrashing occurs when multiple threads frequently evict each other's cached data, leading to excessive memory accesses.

- ❖ Happens when different threads access memory locations that repeatedly invalidate cache lines.

- ❖ Reduces CPU efficiency by forcing frequent main memory fetches instead of leveraging fast cache.

- ❖ Common in high-performance computing, large matrix computations, and deep learning training.

Mitigation Strategies

- ❖ Optimize data locality to ensure threads use cached data efficiently.

- ❖ Reduce unnecessary cache invalidations by aligning memory structures properly.

- ❖ Utilize NUMA-aware memory allocation to minimize cross-core interference.

Question 151 | Concurrency and Parallelism

What is priority inversion in multi-threaded applications, and how can it be prevented ?

Answer

Priority inversion occurs when a low-priority thread holds a resource needed by a higher-priority thread, causing unnecessary blocking.

❖ Real-time systems suffer if critical tasks are delayed due to resource contention.
❖ Operating system schedulers can mismanage priorities, worsening delays.

Mitigation Strategies

❖ Priority inheritance (temporarily raising low-priority thread priority).
❖ Avoid long resource locks by using fine-grained locking.
❖ Monitor thread execution priorities to detect priority inversions early.

>>> Data Structures

Question 152 | Data Structures

How does Python's list implement dynamic resizing, and what is its time complexity for appending elements ?

Answer

Python's list is dynamically resizable, meaning it allocates extra memory when more elements are added beyond its current capacity.

- Uses amortized allocation, resizing by a growth factor (usually ~1.125x or 1.5x in CPython).

Question 153 | Data Structures

What is the difference between tuples and lists in Python, and when should you use tuples instead of lists ?

Answer

Feature	List (list)	Tuple (tuple)
Mutability	Mutable	Immutable
Memory Efficiency	Uses more memory	Uses less memory

Performance	Slower (due to dynamic resizing)	Faster (fixed size)
Hashable	No	Yes (if it contains only immutable elements)

Use tuples instead of lists when

✓ You need immutable data (e.g., function return values, dictionary keys).

✓ You require better performance (tuples have lower overhead).

✓ You need hashability for storing in sets or dictionary keys.

Question 154 | Data Structures

How do Python sets achieve constant-time lookup, and why are they faster than lists for membership testing ?

Answer

Sets (`set`) in Python use a hash table for storage, providing average-case **O(1)** time complexity for lookups.

- ❖ Lists (`list`) require O(n) linear scans for membership tests (in operation).
- ❖ Sets hash elements, ensuring efficient lookups independent of size.

Question 155 | Data Structures

How do Python dictionaries implement key-value storage, and what is their average lookup time complexity ?

Answer

Dictionaries (dict) use hash tables, providing **O(1)** average lookup time complexity.

- ❖ Python's dict maintains insertion order (since Python 3.7+).
- ❖ Uses open addressing for conflict resolution.

Question 156 | Data Structures

How do heaps (heapq) work in Python, and what are their practical applications ?

Answer

A heap (heapq) maintains the smallest element at the root.

✓ Supports efficient min/max operations.
✓ Used for priority queues, scheduling, and graph algorithms.

Operations

- ❖ heappush(heap, item)
- ❖ heappop(heap)

Example Code

```python
import heapq

heap = []
heapq.heappush(heap, 10)
heapq.heappush(heap, 5)
heapq.heappush(heap, 20)
print(heapq.heappop(heap)) # Returns smallest element (5)
```

Heaps ensure efficient priority-based execution for algorithms.

Question 157 | Data Structures

How does Python optimize dictionary (dict) key lookup operations ?

Answer

Python dictionaries achieve **O(1) average lookup time** using **hash tables**.

- ❖ Each key is hashed using a hash function, mapping it to an index in an internal array.

- ❖ If a key's hash collides with another, Python uses open addressing to resolve conflicts.

- ❖ Since insertion order is maintained (Python 3.7+), keys remain predictable.

Question 158 | Data Structures

How does Python's `OrderedDict` differ from `dict`, and when should you use it ?

Answer

OrderedDict maintains insertion order in all Python versions (before 3.7).

✓ It supports ordered iteration, making it ideal for event tracking, caching, and serialization.

✓ Provides additional methods (`move_to_end()`, `popitem(last=True/False)`) for order control.

Question 159 | Data Structures

How does Python implement reference counting for memory management in data structures ?

Answer

Python uses reference counting to manage object lifetime.

❖ Every object maintains a reference count indicating how many variables reference it.

❖ When the count reaches zero, Python automatically deallocates memory.

❖ Circular references are handled using the garbage collector (gc module).

Question 160 | Data Structures

How does Python handle memory fragmentation in dynamic data structures ?

Answer

Python's memory allocator (pymalloc) manages small object allocations, preventing fragmentation.

✓ Frequent insertions/deletions cause memory gaps, reducing cache locality. Best practices

❖ Use preallocated lists instead of frequent `append()` calls.
❖ Leverage deque for dynamic queuing (avoiding list resizing overhead).

Memory optimization enhances efficient access patterns for performance-sensitive applications.

Question 161 | Data Structures

How does Python handle memory fragmentation in dynamic data structures ?

Answer

frozenset is an immutable version of set, meaning elements cannot be modified after creation.

Ideal for

- ❖ Dictionary keys (as sets are mutable and cannot be used).
- ❖ Caching immutable configurations.

>>> Data Engineering & Big Data

Question 162 | Data Engineering and Big Data

What is Apache Airflow ?

Answer

Apache Airflow is an **open-source workflow orchestration tool** that automates ETL pipelines using **Directed Acyclic Graphs (DAGs)**.

Features

- ❖ **Task scheduling & dependency management** – Executes tasks in a **defined order** automatically.

- ❖ **Retries & monitoring** – Automatically **retries failed tasks** and provides **detailed execution logs**.

- ❖ **Parallel execution** – Uses **task concurrency**, scaling ETL workloads efficiently.

- ❖ **Extensible architecture** – Supports **custom plugins** (e.g., KubernetesExecutor, CeleryExecutor).

Example Code

```
from airflow import DAG
from airflow.operators.python import PythonOperator
from datetime import datetime
```

```
def extract():
    print("Extracting data...")

def transform():
    print("Transforming data...")

def load():
    print("Loading data...")

dag = DAG(
    "ETL_Pipeline",
    default_args={"start_date": datetime(2024, 1, 1)},
    schedule_interval="@daily"
)

task1 = PythonOperator(task_id="extract",
python_callable=extract, dag=dag)
task2 = PythonOperator(task_id="transform",
python_callable=transform, dag=dag)
task3 = PythonOperator(task_id="load",
python_callable=load, dag=dag)

task1 >> task2 >> task3  # Defines task dependencies
```

Airflow **optimizes ETL automation by ensuring modular, scalable execution**.

Question 163 | Data Engineering and Big Data

What is the difference between PySpark and Dask for Big Data processing ?

Answer

Feature	PySpark	Dask
Execution Model	Distributed cluster computing	Local and distributed parallel computing
Best Use Case	**Big Data (>TB), production-scale**	**Medium-sized data (~GB), dynamic scaling**
Parallelism	Distributed across nodes	Parallel on multi-core CPUs
Lazy Evaluation	Yes	Yes

PySpark is ideal for large-scale distributed processing, whereas **Dask** provides flexible parallel execution for moderate-sized datasets.

Question 164 | Data Engineering and Big Data

How does PySpark's DataFrame API optimize query execution compared to Pandas ?

Answer

PySpark leverages Catalyst Optimizer, improving query efficiency via

❖ **Predicate pushdown** – Filters are applied **before reading data**, reducing I/O overhead.

❖ **Column pruning** – Retrieves **only required columns**, minimizing memory usage.

❖ **Distributed execution** – Parallelizes tasks across nodes using **RDDs (Resilient Distributed Datasets)**.

Question 165 | Data Engineering and Big Data

How does PySpark handle partitioning in distributed computing, and how does it improve performance ?

Answer

Partitioning splits large datasets across worker nodes, ensuring parallel execution.

Used in

❖ **Shuffling avoidance** → Ensures related data stays close, reducing network I/O.

❖ **Optimized joins** (`.partitionBy()`) → Avoids unnecessary data movement between partitions.

❖ **Cluster-aware execution** → Leverages Spark's **RDD partitioning model**.

Question 166 | Data Engineering and Big Data

What is the difference between wide and narrow

transformations in PySpark ?

Answer

Narrow transformations do not require data movement between partitions (`map()`, `filter()`).

Wide transformations shuffle data across partitions (`groupBy()`, `join()`), causing performance overhead.

Optimizing ETL

- ❖ Reduce wide transformations using **broadcast joins**.

- ❖ Apply narrow transformations **before wide operations** to minimize shuffling.

Question 167 | Data Engineering and Big Data

How do you design a Data Lake architecture in the cloud, and what considerations affect storage, access, and governance ?

Answer

Designing a **Data Lake architecture** in the cloud requires careful planning of **storage layers, access control, and governance policies** to ensure scalable and secure data ingestion and retrieval.

A well-designed Data Lake comprises three key layers

1. **Raw (Bronze) Layer** – Stores unprocessed raw data from various sources like logs, API feeds, transactional databases, and streaming events. Best practices include using scalable object storage (AWS S3, Azure Data Lake, Google Cloud Storage) and applying metadata tagging to track dataset origins.

2. **Processed (Silver) Layer** – Contains cleansed and standardized datasets optimized for analytics. Delta Lake with ACID transactions ensures consistency, preventing issues related to schema evolution.

3. **Curated (Gold) Layer** – Provides fully optimized and aggregated data ready for consumption by analytics tools like Snowflake, Redshift, and BigQuery. This layer supports partitioning, indexing, and efficient data retrieval.

For storage considerations, choosing the right file format plays a critical role in performance. Parquet is preferred for analytics workloads due to its columnar format and efficient compression, while ORC excels in transactional processing. Additionally, versioned storage (using Delta Lake's time-travel feature) enables rollback and historical tracking of data changes.

Access control and security mechanisms must ensure data integrity. Implementing role-based access control (RBAC), fine-grained permissions with IAM policies, and auditing tools like AWS CloudTrail or Azure Monitor provide traceability and prevent unauthorized modifications.

Data governance in a Data Lake is essential to prevent data silos and inconsistencies. Cataloging tools like AWS Glue, Apache Atlas, or Google Data Catalog enable metadata tracking, providing clear visibility into dataset lineage and ensuring compliance with regulations like GDPR and CCPA.

Query optimization in Data Lakes requires techniques like partition pruning, which filters unnecessary partitions, and predicate pushdown, where SQL queries retrieve only relevant rows to reduce computational overhead.

Additionally, cache acceleration with Dremio or Presto enhances interactive query performance for large-scale analytical workloads.

A cloud-based Data Lake must balance scalability, security, governance, and query optimization, ensuring efficient storage and access patterns for modern data engineering pipelines.

Question 168 | Data Engineering and Big Data

What is data modeling, and why is it important in Data Engineering ?

Answer

Data modeling is the process of structuring and organizing data to define relationships, constraints, and retrieval mechanisms for efficient storage and access. It serves as the blueprint for data architecture, ensuring consistency, integrity, and optimized querying across databases and data warehouses.

There are three primary types of data models in data engineering.

1. **Conceptual Data Model** – High-level design describing entity relationships without technical details, used for discussions with business stakeholders.

2. **Logical Data Model** – A structured representation with attributes, relationships, and normalization but without database-specific implementation.

3. **Physical Data Model** – Actual database schema defining tables, indexes, partitions, primary keys, and foreign keys for efficient query execution.

A well-designed data model reduces redundancy, improves retrieval speed, ensures data integrity, and enables scalable storage. For example, in an e-commerce system, a normalized relational model ensures customer orders are linked through foreign keys rather than storing redundant customer data in multiple places.

In Big Data systems, denormalized or schema-less models (e.g. NoSQL, Data Lakes) ensure flexibility by allowing dynamic schema evolution, making them ideal for unstructured or semi-structured data ingestion.

Question 169 | Data Engineering and Big Data

Explain the difference between structured data and unstructured data.

Answer

Structured and unstructured data differ in format, organization, and accessibility.

Structured Data

❖ Stored in tabular format (e.g. relational databases such as PostgreSQL, MySQL).

❖ Has defined schema (e.g. column types, constraints, indexes).

❖ Easily queried using SQL due to its predefined structure.

❖ *Examples are:* Customer transactions, sensor data, financial records.

Unstructured Data

❖ Lacks predefined schema and does not fit into tabular format.

❖ Stored in Data Lakes, NoSQL databases (MongoDB, DynamoDB), or distributed filesystems (HDFS, S3).

❖ Requires natural language processing (NLP), AI, or custom parsing to extract insights.

❖ *Examples are*: Social media posts, emails, images, videos, IoT logs, audio files.

Example Use Case: A company analyzing customer purchase history uses structured data (SQL databases), while analyzing customer reviews or support chats requires processing unstructured data (text analytics, sentiment analysis, keyword extraction).

Structured data fits into traditional databases, while unstructured data requires scalable storage and advanced processing techniques.

Question 170 | Data Engineering and Big Data

What are Big Data's four Vs, and why do they matter ?

Answer

Big Data is characterized by the four Vs

✓ Volume

- ❖ Refers to the massive amount of data generated daily.
- ❖ **Example:** Petabytes of data from social media, sensors, financial transactions.

✓ Velocity

- ❖ Speed at which data is generated and processed in real-time or near real-time.
- ❖ **Example:** Stock market transaction updates, live streaming analytics.

✓ Variety

- ❖ Data comes in multiple formats, structured (SQL databases), semi-structured (JSON, XML), unstructured (videos, logs, tweets).

- ❖ **Example:** Customer behavioral tracking involves logs, purchase data, and social media engagement.

✓ Veracity

- ❖ Ensures data accuracy, consistency, and trustworthiness by removing inconsistencies.

- ❖ **Example:** Cleaning noisy IoT sensor data before analytics to remove errors.

Big Data architectures must handle huge volumes, process high-speed streams, accommodate diverse data types, and ensure reliable data quality for actionable insights.

Question 171 | Data Engineering and Big Data

What is the difference between a data warehouse and an operational database ?

Answer

Data warehouses and operational databases serve different purposes, and their architectures are optimized accordingly.

Data Warehouse

❖ Designed for analytical workloads, stores historical data for reporting and analytics.

❖ Uses OLAP (Online Analytical Processing) for complex queries.

❖ Optimized for read-heavy workloads (e.g. querying trends, forecasting).

❖ Stores denormalized, aggregated data for fast retrieval.

❖ **Examples:** Google BigQuery, Amazon Redshift, Snowflake.

Operational Database

❖ Handles transactional workloads (OLTP - Online Transaction Processing) where frequent inserts, updates, deletes occur.

❖ Optimized for quick response times for CRUD operations (Create, Read, Update, Delete).

❖ Follows normalized schema to prevent duplication and ensure consistency.

❖ **Examples:** MySQL, PostgreSQL, Microsoft SQL Server for banking systems, e-commerce transactions.

Example Scenario

An E-commerce system uses a PostgreSQL operational database for handling user transactions (cart updates, payments), while aggregated sales data is stored in a Snowflake data warehouse for business intelligence dashboards.

Operational databases prioritize fast transactions, while data warehouses optimize analytics at scale.

Question 172 | Data Engineering and Big Data

Designing scalable ETL pipelines.

Answer

Designing scalable ETL pipelines for high-velocity data ingestion requires a distributed processing framework, efficient data partitioning, and incremental processing strategies. In high-velocity environments, data arrives continuously from multiple sources, such as IoT devices, application logs, and API feeds, which must be transformed and stored efficiently without bottlenecks.

Scalability Strategies for ETL Pipelines

✓ Parallel Processing & Task Orchestration

- ❖ Instead of processing data sequentially, ETL pipelines should leverage distributed execution engines like Apache Spark, Dask, or AWS Glue, enabling parallel execution.

❖ Apache Airflow DAGs orchestrate ETL jobs across multiple nodes, ensuring non-blocking workflows.

✓ Incremental Processing Instead of Full Reloads

❖ Instead of processing entire datasets every time, incremental data extraction captures only new or updated records using CDC (Change Data Capture) techniques.

❖ Tools like Debezium track changes in transactional databases and push updates efficiently to ETL pipelines.

✓ Partitioning & Bucketing for Optimized Queries

❖ Data should be partitioned by logical attributes (e.g. timestamp, customer ID, region) to prevent unnecessary scanning.

❖ When writing to cloud storage (AWS S3, Google Cloud Storage), using Parquet or ORC format with partitioned columns improves query efficiency.

✓ Compression & File Format Optimization

❖ Columnar formats (Parquet, ORC) significantly reduce storage space while enabling predicate pushdown, which improves query performance.

❖ Snappy or ZSTD compression reduces I/O overhead and accelerates processing speeds.

✓ Batch vs. Stream Processing Hybrid Approach

❖ Real-time streaming pipelines (Kafka, Spark Streaming) handle high-velocity incoming data with low-latency transformations, while batch jobs process aggregated data periodically.

✓ Scalability Monitoring & Auto-Healing Pipelines

❖ Logging execution times and tracking failures using Datadog, Prometheus, or ELK (Elasticsearch, Logstash, Kibana) enables proactive failure handling and scalability adjustments.

Implementing these optimizations ensures ETL pipelines remain efficient, scalable, and resilient in high-velocity data processing environments.

Question 173 | Data Engineering and Big Data

What are the three main types of data models ?

Answer

Data modeling is the process of defining how data is structured, stored, and interrelated. It is crucial for designing databases, data warehouses, and Big Data architectures.

The **three primary types of data models** are

1. Conceptual Data Model

The conceptual data model provides a high-level view of the data architecture. It is primarily used for discussions with business stakeholders and non-technical teams to define relationships between entities without worrying about database-specific implementation.

❖ Focuses on entity relationships rather than physical table structures.
❖ Does not specify attributes or constraints; instead, it defines major data entities and their interactions.
❖ Commonly represented using Entity-Relationship Diagrams (ERD).

Example

Customer --- places ---> Order --- contains ---> Product

In this representation, entities (Customer, Order, Product) are connected by relationships (places, contains).

2. Logical Data Model

A logical data model is more detailed than a conceptual model and defines specific attributes, relationships, and normalization rules. This model is database-agnostic, meaning it does not depend on any specific database technology.

❖ Defines attributes for each entity (e.g. Customer has Customer_ID, Name, Email).
❖ Enforces normalization to reduce redundancy and improve efficiency.
❖ Primary keys and foreign keys are outlined to establish relationships.

Example (Logical Representation)

```
Customer (Customer_ID, Name, Email)
Order (Order_ID, Date, Customer_ID)
Product (Product_ID, Name, Price)
```

Relationships are expressed through foreign keys, ensuring referential integrity.

3. Physical Data Model

A physical data model translates the logical data model into actual database schema implementation. It defines table structures, indexing strategies, partitioning rules, and storage optimizations.

- ❖ Optimized for database engines (MySQL, PostgreSQL, Snowflake, BigQuery).
- ❖ Includes indexing, partitioning, clustering, and compression techniques to improve query speed.
- ❖ Specifies column data types (VARCHAR, INT, FLOAT) and constraints (e.g. NOT NULL, UNIQUE, CHECK constraints).

Example (Physical Implementation in SQL)

```
CREATE TABLE Customer (
    Customer_ID INT PRIMARY KEY,
    Name VARCHAR(255),
    Email VARCHAR(255) UNIQUE
);
```

Understanding these data model types ensures scalable, optimized database architecture for real-world applications.

Question 174 | Data Engineering and Big Data

What is a Snowflake Schema ?

Answer

A snowflake schema is a normalized database schema used in data warehousing where dimension tables are divided into sub-dimensions, reducing data duplication.

Characteristics of a Snowflake Schema

✓ Normalization (higher than Star Schema) – Dimension tables are split into hierarchical sub-tables (e.g. Location → Country → Region).

✓ Reduced storage redundancy – Ensures data consistency but increases join complexity.

✓ Optimized for complex analytics – Useful for BI tools that require structured data retrieval.

Advantages of Snowflake Schema

✓ **Reduces redundancy** and improves data integrity.
✓ **Efficient for analytical queries** needing structured dimensions.
✓ **Optimized for cloud-based warehouses (Snowflake, BigQuery, Redshift)**.

Disadvantages

✓ **Complex join operations** increase computational overhead.
✓ **Not ideal for high-speed queries**, since multiple joins are required.

A snowflake schema is best for highly structured and normalized data environments where storage efficiency is prioritized.

Question 175 | Data Engineering and Big Data

What is a Star Schema ?

Answer

A star schema is a denormalized schema commonly used in data warehouses, where a central fact table is connected to multiple dimension tables in a star-like structure.

Key Characteristics of a Star Schema

✓ **Denormalized structure** – Dimension tables store repeated values to reduce joins.

✓ **Optimized for fast query performance** – Best for OLAP (Online Analytical Processing) workloads.

✓ **Less complex joins** – Compared to snowflake schema, query execution is faster.

Question 176 | Data Engineering and Big Data

What is Batch Processing ?

Answer

Batch processing refers to the execution of data processing tasks in large groups (batches) at scheduled intervals, instead of processing data in real time.

How Batch Processing Works

✓ Data is collected over time and processed in bulk periodically.

✓ Used for ETL jobs, reporting, historical analytics, and data transformations.

✓ Often scheduled using Apache Airflow, AWS Batch, or Hadoop MapReduce.

Example of a Batch Processing Pipeline

1. **Extract** - Load data from databases (MySQL, PostgreSQL).

2. **Transform** - Perform aggregations, cleaning (deduplication, normalization).

3. **Load** - Store processed data into a warehouse (Snowflake, Redshift).

Question 177 | Data Engineering and Big Data

Explain the concept of data partitioning ?

Answer

Data partitioning is the process of splitting large datasets into smaller, more manageable sections to optimize query performance and reduce processing time.

Types of Data Partitioning

✓ **Horizontal Partitioning** – Divides rows into segments based on attributes (e.g. partition by date, customer ID).

✓ **Vertical Partitioning** – Splits tables by columns to store frequently accessed attributes separately (used in columnar databases).

✓ **Range Partitioning** – Assigns rows to partitions based on a defined range (e.g. Partitioning transactions by year).

Example of Partitioned Storage in BigQuery

```
CREATE TABLE sales_partitioned (
    transaction_id STRING,
    product_name STRING,
    sales_amount FLOAT,
    transaction_date DATE
)
PARTITION BY transaction_date;
```

Partitioning reduces I/O overhead, ensuring queries process only relevant partitions instead of scanning the entire dataset.

>>> **Cloud and DevOps**

_____

Question 178 | Cloud and DevOps

How does Infrastructure as Code (IaC) work with Python, and how do tools like Terraform and Ansible automate cloud provisioning ?

Answer

Infrastructure as Code (IaC) enables DevOps teams to define and deploy infrastructure using declarative code, ensuring consistency and scalability across cloud environments.

Python integrates with IaC tools like Terraform and Ansible, allowing developers to automate provisioning, configuration, and orchestration of cloud infrastructure.

Terraform and Python (Provisioning Cloud Resources)

Terraform uses declarative HashiCorp Configuration Language (HCL), but Python can automate Terraform execution via wrapper libraries.

Question 179 | Cloud and DevOps

How do you ensure high availability and fault tolerance in Python-based cloud applications deployed on Kubernetes ?

Answer

High availability and fault tolerance in Python-based cloud applications deployed on Kubernetes require strategic replication, load balancing, auto-scaling, and recovery mechanisms to prevent outages and ensure reliability.

High Availability Strategies in Kubernetes

1. **Replica Sets for Redundancy**

    a. Kubernetes automatically maintains multiple instances of a Python application, ensuring that a failure does not cause downtime.

    b. A ReplicaSet definition specifies the number of pod replicas that should always be running.

2. **Load Balancing with Kubernetes Services**

    a. Kubernetes routes requests evenly across multiple pods using ClusterIP (internal), NodePort (external), or LoadBalancer (cloud provider-specific).

    b. **Example:** Load balancing a Python Flask app across multiple pods.

3. **Auto-Scaling Using Horizontal Pod Autoscaler (HPA)**

    a. If the application experiences high CPU or memory utilization, Kubernetes automatically scales up the number of pods.

    b. HPA ensures elastic scaling, dynamically adjusting based on demand.

Fault-Tolerant Strategies in Kubernetes

1. **Rolling Updates & Canary Deployments**

   a. Kubernetes gradually replaces old versions with new ones using rolling updates, minimizing downtime.

   b. Canary deployments introduce new versions gradually, reducing impact if an issue occurs.

2. **Health Checks and Self-Healing Mechanisms**

   a. Liveness probes ensure unhealthy pods are restarted, preventing failures.

   b. Readiness probes ensure traffic is only routed to pods ready to serve requests.

Question 180 | Cloud and DevOps

How do Python-based DevOps workflows integrate with cloud monitoring and logging solutions to improve observability ?

Answer

Observability in Python-based cloud applications is achieved through logging, monitoring, tracing, and alerting systems that provide real-time insights into performance, failures, and bottlenecks.

Logging Solutions for Python in the Cloud

1. **Cloud Logging Services (AWS CloudWatch, Google Cloud Logging, Azure Monitor)**

    a. Capture application logs, aggregate errors, and track execution traces.

    b. Python integrates with these services via SDKs (boto3, google-cloud-sdk, azure-monitor).

2. **Centralized Logging with ELK Stack (Elasticsearch, Logstash, Kibana)**

    a. Logs are ingested via Logstash, stored in Elasticsearch, and visualized in Kibana dashboards.

    b. Ensures searchable, structured log analytics.

Monitoring and Metrics Collection in Python Applications

1. **Prometheus and Grafana for Cloud Metrics**

    a. Prometheus scrapes metrics from Python applications, while Grafana visualizes performance trends.

    b. Monitor API response times, database latency, and CPU/memory usage.

2. **Tracing Requests in Distributed Systems Using OpenTelemetry**

    a. OpenTelemetry traces requests across microservices, ensuring bottlenecks are identified.

    b. Helps diagnose failures in cloud-based distributed applications.

Question 181 | Cloud and DevOps

How do you ensure continuous monitoring and auto-scaling for Python-based applications in cloud environments ?

Answer

Continuous monitoring and auto-scaling in Python-based cloud applications ensure that systems remain responsive, efficient, and cost-effective under varying loads. Cloud providers like AWS, Google Cloud, and Azure offer built-in monitoring and auto-scaling services, which can be integrated directly into Python applications.

1. Continuous Monitoring Using Cloud-Native Tools

Monitoring involves tracking CPU utilization, memory usage, network activity, error logs, and application performance metrics.

Cloud platforms provide several monitoring tools

❖ AWS CloudWatch monitors Python application logs, resource utilization, and metrics, sending automated alerts in case of anomalies.

❖ Google Cloud Operations Suite (formerly Stackdriver) tracks application performance and identifies slow database queries.

❖ Azure Monitor and Application Insights enable real-time logging and alerting for performance bottlenecks.

2. Auto-Scaling to Handle Dynamic Workloads

Auto-scaling ensures cloud applications adjust computing resources dynamically based on demand. Kubernetes uses the Horizontal Pod Autoscaler (HPA) to automatically scale services when CPU or memory utilization exceeds a threshold.

Question 182 | Cloud and DevOps

How does Kubernetes ensure container orchestration for Python applications, and what are its advantages ?

Answer

Kubernetes manages Python containerized applications by providing automatic scaling, load balancing, and deployment orchestration across cloud environments.

Key Kubernetes Components for Python Applications

1. **Pods** – The smallest deployable unit, containing one or multiple containers.

2. **Deployments** – Define **replica count, rolling updates, and self-healing policies**.

3. **Services** – Expose Python applications internally or externally.

4. **Ingress Controllers** – Manage **external HTTP routing** for web applications.

Advantages of Using Kubernetes for Python Applications

1. **Automatic Scaling** – Kubernetes adjusts the number of running pods dynamically.

2. **Fault Tolerance** – If a pod fails, Kubernetes automatically restarts it, ensuring uptime.

3. **Load Balancing** – Kubernetes distributes traffic across replicas efficiently.

4. **Rolling Updates** – New versions of Python applications can be gradually deployed without downtime.

Question 183 | Cloud and DevOps

What is the difference between Continuous Integration (CI), Continuous Delivery (CD), and Continuous Deployment ?

Answer

Continuous Integration (CI), Continuous Delivery (CD), and Continuous Deployment are core concepts in DevOps that automate the build, test, and deployment process.

❖ **Continuous Integration (CI)** – Developers push changes to a shared repository multiple times a day, triggering automated builds and tests. CI ensures that code quality remains high and reduces integration conflicts.

❖ **Continuous Delivery (CD)** – After CI, the tested code is automatically packaged and prepared for deployment. The system remains ready to be deployed manually at any time.

❖ **Continuous Deployment** – The final step, where every validated code change is automatically deployed to production, eliminating manual intervention.

Question 184 | Cloud and DevOps

How do you implement blue-green deployments in cloud environments, and why are they beneficial ?

Answer

Blue-Green deployment is a strategy to minimize downtime and risk when releasing new versions of an application.

How Blue-Green Deployments Work

1. **Two Identical Production Environments (Blue & Green)**

   a. The Blue environment serves live traffic.

   b. The Green environment hosts the new application version for validation.

2. **Traffic Switching via Load Balancer**
   a. Once validated, traffic is redirected from Blue to Green, ensuring instant rollback if issues arise.

Why Blue-Green Deployment is Beneficial ?

1. **Zero Downtime Upgrades** – Users experience no disruption during updates.

2. **Instant Rollback Capability** – If Green fails, the load balancer switches back to Blue, preventing downtime.

3. **Reduces Deployment Risk** – Parallel environments allow pre-release testing.·

Question 185 | Cloud and DevOps

How does Python integrate with cloud-native monitoring solutions like Prometheus and ELK Stack ?

Answer

Python interacts with Prometheus and ELK Stack (Elasticsearch, Logstash, Kibana) to provide real-time monitoring and log analysis for cloud applications.

How Prometheus Works for Metrics Collection

1. **Python applications expose** /metrics **endpoints**.

2. **Prometheus scrapes metrics** and stores them in a time-series database.

3. **Grafana visualizes application health and trends**.

How ELK Stack Works for Log Analysis

★ **Elasticsearch** indexes structured logs.

- ★ **Logstash** processes application logs.
- ★ **Kibana** visualizes log trends.

Question 186 | Cloud and DevOps

What are some common tools used in DevOps for CI/CD pipelines ?

Answer

DevOps relies on various tools to automate CI/CD workflows

1. **Jenkins** – Open-source automation server for CI/CD.

2. **GitHub Actions** – Native CI/CD integration with GitHub repositories.

3. **GitLab CI/CD** – Built-in CI/CD pipelines for GitLab projects.

4. **CircleCI** – Cloud-based CI/CD automation.

5. **ArgoCD** – Kubernetes-native continuous deployment tool.

Question 187 | Cloud and DevOps

What is the difference between Virtual Machines (VMs) and Docker containers ?

Answer

Virtual Machines (VMs) and Docker containers are both virtualization technologies, but they differ in architecture, resource allocation, and use cases.

1. Architecture Differences

VMs (Virtual Machines)

❖ A VM emulates an entire operating system (OS) on a hypervisor, allowing multiple OS instances to run on the same physical machine.

❖ Each VM has its own dedicated OS kernel, drivers, and libraries, creating complete isolation between instances.

❖ Examples of hypervisors: VMware, Hyper-V, VirtualBox, KVM.

Docker (Containers)

❖ Docker virtualizes at the application level, meaning containers share the host OS kernel rather than running separate OS instances.

❖ Containers are lightweight, start quickly, and only contain the necessary libraries and dependencies, making them more efficient.

2. Resource Consumption

VMs

❖ Require more CPU, memory, and storage because each VM runs a full OS.

❖ Start-up time is slow, often taking minutes due to OS booting.

Docker

❖ Uses less system resources because it shares the host OS kernel.

❖ Containers start within seconds, making them ideal for microservices and cloud deployments.

3. Isolation and Security

VMs

❖ VMs offer stronger isolation since each runs a full OS, reducing security risks from the host system.
❖ Preferred for hosting legacy applications and multi-tenant environments.

Docker

❖ Containers share the host OS, making them less isolated than VMs but more efficient for rapid deployments.
❖ Security vulnerabilities can impact the host OS, but mitigations like Kubernetes RBAC and AppArmor help reduce risks.

4. Use Cases

VMs

❖ Ideal for running multiple operating systems (Linux on Windows, Windows on macOS).
❖ Used for traditional applications that require full OS environments.
❖ Preferred for enterprise IT virtualization and cloud hosting.

Docker

❖ Best for containerized microservices that need fast scaling and automation.
❖ Ideal for CI/CD pipelines, cloud-native applications, and Kubernetes clusters.

❖ Used extensively in DevOps environments for software deployment and testing.

Conclusion

VMs provide full OS virtualization, offering strong isolation but higher resource usage, while Docker virtualizes applications using shared OS kernels, making it lighter, faster, and more efficient for cloud-native workloads.

>>> Security

Question 188 | Security

How do you implement encryption in Python using PyCryptodome, and why is it essential for data protection ?

Answer

Why Encryption is Important

1. **Protects sensitive user data** (e.g. passwords, financial transactions).
2. **Prevents data leaks and unauthorized access** in storage and transmission.
3. **Ensures compliance** with security regulations like **GDPR and HIPAA**.

Example: **Implementing AES Encryption Using PyCryptodome**

AES (**Advanced Encryption Standard**) is a widely used symmetric encryption algorithm.

Example Code

```
from Crypto.Cipher import AES
import os

# Generate random 16-byte key
key = os.urandom(16)
cipher = AES.new(key, AES.MODE_EAX)
```

```
# Encrypt the data
plaintext = b"Sensitive Data"
ciphertext, tag = cipher.encrypt_and_digest(plaintext)

# Store the nonce to decrypt later
nonce = cipher.nonce

print(f"Encrypted Data: {ciphertext.hex()}")

# Decryption process
cipher = AES.new(key, AES.MODE_EAX, nonce=nonce)
decrypted_text = cipher.decrypt(ciphertext)

print(f"Decrypted Data: {decrypted_text.decode()}")
```

Question 189 | Security

What are some real-life security incidents in Python applications, and how were they resolved ?

Answer

Real-world Python security incidents have highlighted **major vulnerabilities** and how companies fixed them.

1. Instagram API Exposure (2018)

- **Issue** – Attackers exploited Instagram's API rate limits to brute-force user login credentials.

- **Resolution** – Instagram implemented stricter authentication mechanisms, enforced rate-limiting, and introduced OAuth for API access.

2. Equifax Data Breach (2017)

- **Issue** – Sensitive customer data was leaked due to poor input sanitization in a Python web application.

- **Resolution** – Equifax implemented strict validation for API payloads, enforced web application firewalls, and improved logging & monitoring.

3. Capital One AWS S3 Leak (2019)

- **Issue** – Misconfigured S3 permissions allowed unauthorized access to sensitive data.

- **Resolution** – Capital One tightened IAM roles, introduced encryption at rest, and enforced IAM policy audits.

Lessons Learned

- Always validate inputs to prevent injection attacks.
- Use proper authentication mechanisms (OAuth, JWT).
- Encrypt sensitive user data before storing it in cloud databases.
- Restrict API access & enforce rate limiting to prevent brute-force attacks.

Real-life security incidents show **the importance of proactive security practices**, preventing **major breaches and reputation damage**.

Question 190 | Security

What is authentication in web applications ?

Answer

Authentication is the process of verifying a user's identity before granting access to a web application. Secure authentication ensures that unauthorized users cannot gain access to sensitive resources or perform actions they are not permitted to. In Python-based web applications, authentication can be implemented using frameworks like Flask, Django, or FastAPI, with various security techniques to protect user credentials.

A common method of authentication is password-based login, where users provide a username and password. Passwords should never be stored in plaintext; instead, they must be hashed using strong hashing algorithms such as bcrypt or Argon2. Python's hashlib and bcrypt libraries can be used for secure password hashing.

Multi-factor authentication (MFA) enhances security by requiring users to verify their identity using an additional factor beyond their password, such as an OTP (one-time password) generated via TOTP (Time-Based One-Time Password). Libraries like pyotp enable MFA implementation in Python applications, providing an extra layer of security.

OAuth 2.0 and JSON Web Tokens (JWT) are widely used for authentication in APIs. OAuth allows users to authenticate via third-party providers like Google, GitHub, or Facebook without managing passwords directly. JWTs store authentication claims in signed tokens, reducing the need for session-based authentication while ensuring secure user validation.

To protect authentication mechanisms, rate limiting should be enforced to prevent brute force attacks, and HTTPS must be used to encrypt data transmission. Secure session management ensures that user sessions expire appropriately and tokens cannot be reused maliciously.

Question 191 | Security

What is the difference between authentication and authorization, and why are both necessary for security ?

Answer

Authentication verifies a user's identity, ensuring that they are who they claim to be, while authorization determines what actions they are allowed to perform once authenticated. Both are necessary for security because authentication alone does not enforce access control. Without authorization, authenticated users could access restricted resources or perform operations beyond their intended privileges.

In Python web applications, authentication is handled through login mechanisms like username/password validation, OAuth, or biometric authentication. Authorization is enforced through role-based access control (RBAC), where users are assigned specific roles that dictate their permissions.

For example, in a banking application, authentication ensures that a user logging in is legitimate. Authorization ensures that a customer can view their account balance but cannot modify another customer's data or access administrative controls reserved for employees.

Properly implemented authentication and authorization prevent unauthorized access, data leaks, and privilege escalation attacks, ensuring that users can only perform actions aligned with their permissions.

Question 192 | Security

What is the difference between symmetric and asymmetric encryption ?

Answer

Symmetric encryption uses a single key for both encryption and decryption, meaning the same key must be securely shared between the sender and receiver. This method is efficient and fast, making it ideal for encrypting large amounts of data. Common symmetric encryption algorithms include AES (Advanced Encryption Standard) and DES (Data Encryption Standard).

Asymmetric encryption, on the other hand, uses a pair of keys: a public key for encryption and a private key for decryption. This eliminates the need for secure key exchange, as the public key can be freely distributed while the private key remains confidential. Asymmetric encryption is commonly used for secure communications, digital signatures, and key exchange protocols. RSA (Rivest-Shamir-Adleman) and ECC (Elliptic Curve Cryptography) are widely used asymmetric encryption algorithms.

Symmetric encryption is best suited for encrypting large datasets, such as database records or file storage, due to its speed and efficiency. Asymmetric encryption is preferred for secure authentication, digital signatures, and encrypting small amounts of data, such as passwords or API keys.

In practice, both encryption types are often combined, symmetric encryption secures bulk data, while asymmetric encryption is used to securely exchange symmetric keys.

Question 193 | Security

What are common API security vulnerabilities ?

Answer

APIs are vulnerable to various security threats, including unauthorized access, injection attacks, and data leaks. Common API security vulnerabilities include:

1. **Broken Authentication** – If authentication mechanisms are weak, attackers can gain unauthorized access. APIs should enforce strong authentication using OAuth 2.0 or JWT (JSON Web Tokens).

2. **Injection Attacks** – APIs that accept user input without validation are susceptible to SQL injection or command injection. Input sanitization and parameterized queries prevent these attacks.

3. **Excessive Data Exposure** – APIs should only return necessary data. Overexposing sensitive information in API responses can lead to data leaks.

4. **Rate Limiting and Throttling** – APIs should enforce request limits to prevent abuse and brute-force attacks. Flask-Limiter or Django Throttling can be used to implement rate limiting.

5. **HTTPS Enforcement** – APIs must use TLS encryption (https://) to prevent man-in-the-middle attacks.

Question 194 | Security

What is the role of hashing in security ?

Answer

Hashing is a cryptographic technique used to generate a fixed-length representation of data, ensuring integrity and authenticity. Unlike encryption, which transforms data into ciphertext that can be decrypted, hashing is a one-way function, once data is hashed, it cannot be reversed to its original form. This makes hashing ideal for storing passwords, verifying file integrity, and ensuring data authenticity.

A common use case for hashing is password storage. Instead of storing plaintext passwords, applications hash passwords using algorithms like **SHA-256, bcrypt, or Argon2**. When a user logs in, their entered password is hashed and compared to the stored hash. If they match, authentication is successful.

Question 195 | Security

What is the principle of least privilege ?

Answer

The principle of least privilege **(PoLP)** is a security concept that ensures users, applications, and processes have only the minimum permissions necessary to perform their tasks. This reduces the risk of unauthorized access, privilege escalation, and security breaches.

In Python applications, PoLP is enforced by restricting access to sensitive resources, databases, and APIs. For example, instead of granting full administrative privileges to an API key, developers should assign role-based access controls (RBAC) to limit actions.

For cloud-based applications, IAM policies should be configured to grant only necessary permissions.

Question 196 | Security

How do you implement secure session management in Python web applications ?

Answer

Session management is used for maintaining user authentication and preventing unauthorized access. Poor session management can lead to session hijacking, fixation, and replay attacks, compromising user security.

To implement secure session management in Python web applications:

1. **Use secure session tokens** – generate cryptographically strong session IDs using UUID or JWT.

2. **Set session expiration** – ensure that sessions expire after a defined period to prevent prolonged access.

3. **Store session data securely** – use encrypted cookies or server-side storage instead of exposing session data in URLs.

4. **Enforce HTTPS** – encrypt session data in transit to prevent interception.

Question 197 | Security

How do you prevent timing attacks in Python applications, and why are they a security concern ?

Answer

Timing attacks occur when an attacker measures the time taken by a system to process different inputs, allowing them to infer sensitive information such as cryptographic keys or authentication tokens. These attacks exploit variations in execution time to deduce whether certain conditions are met, making them particularly dangerous in cryptographic operations and password validation.

In Python applications, timing attacks can occur when comparing sensitive data, such as password hashes or authentication tokens. A common mistake is using the `==` operator for string comparisons, which may return results faster for certain inputs, revealing information about the underlying data.

For example, the following code is vulnerable to timing attacks

```
def insecure_compare(input_token, stored_token):
    return input_token == stored_token
```

To prevent timing attacks, developers should use constant-time comparison functions, which ensure that execution time remains uniform regardless of input differences.

Python's `hmac.compare_digest()` provides a secure way to compare sensitive data:

```
import hmac

def secure_compare(input_token, stored_token):
    return hmac.compare_digest(input_token, stored_token)
# Prevents timing attacks
```

By using constant-time comparison functions, Python applications can prevent attackers from deducing sensitive information based on execution time variations, ensuring secure authentication and cryptographic operations.

Question 198 | Security

How do you prevent brute-force attacks ?

Answer

Brute-force attacks occur when an attacker systematically tries different combinations of passwords or authentication tokens to gain unauthorized access to an application. These attacks can be automated using scripts that rapidly test thousands or millions of credentials, making them a significant security concern for web applications, APIs, and login systems.

To prevent brute-force attacks, Python applications should implement rate limiting, account lockouts, and multi-factor authentication (MFA). Rate limiting restricts the number of login attempts a user can make within a specific timeframe, preventing automated attacks. Flask-Limiter or Django Throttling can be used to enforce rate limits in Python applications.

Account lockouts temporarily disable user accounts after multiple failed login attempts, preventing attackers from repeatedly guessing passwords.

This can be implemented by tracking failed login attempts and locking the account after a predefined threshold.

Multi-factor authentication (MFA) adds an extra layer of security by requiring users to verify their identity using an additional factor beyond their password, such as an OTP (one-time password) sent via email or SMS. Python's pyotp library enables MFA implementation, ensuring that even if an attacker obtains a password, they cannot access the account without the second authentication factor.

By enforcing rate limiting, account lockouts, and MFA, Python applications can effectively prevent brute-force attacks, ensuring secure authentication and user protection.

Question 199 | Security

How do you secure Python applications against man-in-the-middle (MITM) attacks, and why are they dangerous ?

Answer

Man-in-the-middle (MITM) attacks occur when an attacker intercepts communication between two parties, allowing them to eavesdrop, modify, or steal sensitive data. These attacks are particularly dangerous in applications that transmit authentication credentials, financial transactions, or confidential information over unsecured networks.

To secure Python applications against MITM attacks, developers should enforce TLS encryption, implement certificate pinning, and use secure authentication mechanisms.

Certificate pinning prevents attackers from using fraudulent certificates to impersonate legitimate services. By hardcoding trusted certificates, applications can reject unauthorized certificates during authentication.

Secure authentication mechanisms, such as OAuth 2.0 and mutual TLS authentication, ensure that only verified clients can establish connections.

By enforcing TLS encryption, certificate pinning, and secure authentication, Python applications can prevent MITM attacks, ensuring that sensitive data remains protected during transmission.

Question 200 | Security

How do you secure Python applications against SQL injection in NoSQL databases ?

Answer

SQL injection is commonly associated with relational databases, but NoSQL databases like MongoDB and Firebase are also vulnerable to injection attacks. Attackers can manipulate NoSQL queries to retrieve unauthorized data or modify database records.

To prevent NoSQL injection, Python applications should use parameterized queries, validate user input, and enforce access controls. MongoDB's pymongo library provides secure query mechanisms that prevent injection attacks.

>>> Optimization

Question 201 | Optimization

What is the difference between time complexity and space complexity in Python optimization, and why are both important ?

Answer

Time complexity refers to the amount of time an algorithm takes to execute as a function of the input size, while space complexity refers to the amount of memory an algorithm consumes during execution. Both are crucial in Python optimization because they determine the efficiency of a program, especially when dealing with large datasets or computationally intensive tasks.

Time complexity is measured using Big-O notation, which describes the worst-case scenario of an algorithm's growth rate.

For example, an algorithm with $O(n)$ complexity grows linearly with input size, while $O(n^2)$ complexity grows quadratically, making it significantly slower for large inputs.

Space complexity, on the other hand, considers how much memory is allocated for variables, data structures, and recursive calls. An algorithm that requires $O(1)$ space is considered optimal because it uses a constant amount of memory regardless of input size, whereas $O(n)$ space complexity increases proportionally with input size.

Optimizing both time and space complexity ensures that Python applications run efficiently, avoiding excessive computation time and memory usage. Techniques such as memoization, efficient data structures, and algorithmic improvements help reduce complexity and improve performance.

Question 202 | Optimization

How does Python's built-in data structures impact performance optimization, and when should you use lists, sets, or dictionaries ?

Answer

Python's built-in data structures – lists, sets, and dictionaries play a crucial role in performance optimization by providing efficient ways to store and manipulate data. Choosing the right data structure can significantly improve execution speed and memory usage.

Lists are dynamic arrays that allow fast indexing **(O(1))** but slow insertions and deletions **(O(n))** when modifying elements in the middle. They are ideal for ordered collections where frequent indexing is required.

Sets provide **O(1)** average-time complexity for membership checks and eliminate duplicate values automatically. They are useful when checking for unique elements or performing fast lookups.

Dictionaries use hash tables to store key-value pairs, offering **O(1)** average-time complexity for lookups, insertions, and deletions. They are optimal for mapping relationships between data points, such as storing configurations or caching results.

Choosing the appropriate data structure based on the operation type ensures efficient execution.

For example, using a dictionary instead of a list for frequent lookups can drastically reduce execution time, making Python applications more performant.

Question 203 | Optimization

What is vectorization in Python, and how does it optimize numerical computations ?

Answer

Vectorization is an optimization technique that replaces explicit loops with array-based operations, significantly improving performance in numerical computations. Python libraries like NumPy and Pandas provide built-in vectorized functions that execute operations efficiently using low-level optimizations.

Question 204 | Optimization

What is loop unrolling ?

Answer

Loop unrolling is an optimization technique that reduces loop overhead by executing multiple iterations within a single loop cycle. This minimizes branching and improves execution speed, especially in computationally intensive tasks.

For example, instead of iterating through a loop one step at a time

```
for i in range(1000):
    process(i)
```

Loop unrolling executes multiple iterations per cycle

```
for i in range(0, 1000, 4):
    process(i)
    process(i+1)
    process(i+2)
    process(i+3)
```

While Python does not automatically unroll loops, developers can manually apply this technique to optimize performance in numerical computations and data processing.

Question 205 | Optimization

What is branch prediction ?

Answer

Branch prediction is a CPU optimization technique that anticipates the outcome of conditional statements (if-else) to minimize execution delays.

While Python does not directly control branch prediction, writing efficient conditional logic can improve performance.

Question 206 | Optimization

How does Python's numba library improve performance, and when should it be used ?

Answer

Numba is a Just-In-Time (JIT) compiler for Python that accelerates numerical computations by compiling Python functions into optimized machine code. It is particularly useful for speeding up loops and mathematical operations without requiring extensive code modifications.

Numba works by applying the `@jit` decorator to functions, enabling automatic compilation:

```
from numba import jit

@jit(nopython=True)
def compute_squares(n):
    result = []
    for i in range(n):
        result.append(i**2)
    return result

print(compute_squares(1000000))  # Faster execution
```

Numba is ideal for optimizing scientific computing, machine learning, and data analysis tasks where performance is critical. It significantly improves execution speed compared to standard Python loops.

Question 207 | Optimization

What is string interning, and how does it optimize performance ?

Answer

String interning is a performance optimization technique where Python stores identical immutable strings in a single memory location, reducing memory usage and speeding up string comparisons. This is particularly useful for frequently used strings, such as variable names and dictionary keys.

Python automatically interns short strings and identifiers, meaning that identical strings share the same memory reference.

Question 208 | Optimization

How does Python optimize integer storage using integer caching ?

Answer

Python optimizes integer storage by caching frequently used small integers (-5 to 256), ensuring that identical integers share the same memory reference. This reduces memory usage and speeds up integer operations. String

Question 209 | Optimization

How is Peephole optimization ?

Answer

Peephole optimization is a technique used by Python's interpreter to optimize bytecode by eliminating redundant operations and simplifying expressions. This optimization occurs at the bytecode level, improving execution speed without modifying source code.

Similarly, Python removes unnecessary jumps and redundant instructions in loops and conditionals, ensuring efficient execution. Peephole optimization enhances performance by reducing bytecode complexity, making Python programs run faster.

Question 210 | Optimization

What is Python's zero-cost exception handling ?

Answer

Python implements zero-cost exception handling, meaning that defining try-except blocks does not introduce performance overhead unless an exception is actually raised. Unlike some languages where exception handling incurs runtime costs, Python optimizes exception handling by maintaining a separate exception state that does not affect normal execution flow.

Question 211 | Optimization

What is fast argument passing ?

Answer

Fast argument passing in Python refers to optimizations in how function arguments are handled to reduce overhead and improve execution speed. Python uses efficient memory management techniques to pass arguments, ensuring minimal performance impact.

How Python Passes Arguments

Python follows a call-by-object-sharing model, meaning function arguments are passed as references to objects rather than copying values. This reduces memory usage and speeds up function calls, especially for large data structures.

Question 212 | Optimization

What is the __slots__ and how does it optimize attribute lookup ?

Answer

In Python, class instances typically store attributes in a dictionary (__dict__), which allows dynamic attribute creation but consumes more memory. The __slots__ attribute provides an optimization by restricting attribute storage to a predefined set, eliminating the need for a __dict__ and improving memory efficiency.

How __slots__ works

By defining __slots__ in a class, Python replaces the default dictionary-based attribute storage with a more compact structure, reducing memory overhead and speeding up attribute access.

Benefits of Using __slots__

1. **Memory Efficiency** – Instances use a more compact structure instead of a dictionary, reducing memory footprint.

2. **Faster Attribute Lookup** – Avoids dictionary key lookups, making attribute access faster.

3. **Prevents Accidental Attribute Creation** – Restricts attributes to predefined names, preventing unintended modifications.

4. **Improves Performance in Large-Scale Applications** – Particularly useful when creating thousands or millions of instances.

Limitations of __slots__

1. **No Dynamic Attribute Addition** – Instances cannot have attributes outside the defined __slots__.

2. **No __dict__ or __weakref__** – If __slots__ is used, instances do not support weak references unless explicitly included.

3. **Limited Use in Multiple Inheritance** – __slots__ can cause conflicts when used in multiple-inheritance scenarios

When to Use __slots__

1. When creating **large numbers of instances** (e.g. data processing, simulations).

2. When **memory optimization** is critical.

3. When **attribute lookup speed** is a priority.

>>> Soft Skills

Question 213 | Soft Skills

How do you handle debugging and troubleshooting complex Python issues ?

Answer

Suggested Answer Approach

- Explain how you use debugging tools like pdb, logging, or profiling (cProfile for performance issues).

- Demonstrate a structured approach, such as reproducing the issue, isolating the root cause, and applying fixes with minimal side effects.

- Mention best practices like writing unit tests or using exception handling to prevent similar issues.

Example statement: *"I typically start by reproducing the issue under controlled conditions to pinpoint the cause. For performance bottlenecks, I use cProfile to analyze slow functions, and for logical errors, I rely on logging and debugging tools like pdb. Additionally, I ensure fixes don't introduce new issues by writing unit tests."*

Question 214 | Soft Skills

How do you collaborate with other developers in a project ?

Answer

Suggested Answer Approach

- Mention how you use Git for version control and best practices like branching (feature branches, pull requests).

- Discuss code reviews as a way to share knowledge and maintain consistency.

- Highlight how documentation (README, API specs, inline comments) improves collaboration.

Example statement: *"I ensure collaboration by following Git best practices and maintaining clear documentation. Code reviews are essential for quality, and I engage in technical discussions to improve project design. Regular stand-ups help align the team and prevent blockers."*

Question 215 | Soft Skills

What steps do you take to ensure code quality ?

Answer

Suggested Answer Approach

- Mention linters (flake8, black), static analysis tools, and unit testing (pytest).

- Discuss modular code design following SOLID principles.

- Talk about performance optimizations, ensuring efficient memory use and avoiding redundant operations.

- Code review/crafting with AI Tools

Example statement: *"I ensure code quality through consistent formatting, unit testing (pytest), and adhering to Pythonic best practices like DRY and SOLID principles. Regular refactoring improves maintainability while profiling tools help optimize performance."*

Question 216 | Soft Skills

How do you handle constructive criticism in code reviews ?

Answer

Suggested Answer Approach

- Show openness to feedback and willingness to learn.

- Discuss how you use code reviews to enhance best practices.

- Mention how you handle disagreements professionally (data-driven discussions).

Example statement: *"I treat code reviews as learning opportunities. When receiving feedback, I evaluate its relevance and ask clarifying questions when needed. I apply suggested improvements while ensuring they align with project goals. Technical discussions help refine solutions."*

Question 217 | Soft Skills

How do you handle unexpected project changes or shifting requirements ?

Answer

Suggested Answer Approach

- Demonstrate adaptability using Agile methodologies (scrum, sprints).

- Show proactive problem-solving, ensuring flexibility while minimizing disruption.

- Highlight how clear communication with stakeholders helps manage expectations.

Example statement: *"I approach unexpected changes using Agile techniques – breaking down adjustments into manageable tasks while keeping the bigger project vision intact. I prioritize open communication with stakeholders to align expectations."*

Question 218 | Soft Skills

How do you handle working under tight deadlines ?

Answer

Suggested Answer Approach

- Explain time management techniques (Pomodoro method, prioritization strategies).

- Highlight how you streamline development using automation and efficient workflows.

- Demonstrate ability to maintain quality without compromising speed.

Example statement: *"I handle deadlines by breaking tasks into achievable milestones and leveraging automation tools. I focus on delivering high-impact changes first while ensuring code remains efficient and maintainable. Communicating proactively with teams helps prevent last-minute issues."*

Question 219 | Soft Skills

How do you handle ambiguity in project requirements ?

Answer

Suggested Answer Approach

- Explain how you seek clarification from stakeholders or product owners.

- Mention how you use prototyping or incremental development to refine unclear requirements.

- Highlight adaptability and problem-solving skills in uncertain situations.

Example statement: *"When faced with ambiguous requirements, I first seek clarification from stakeholders. If details remain unclear, I create a prototype or proof-of-concept to validate assumptions. I also document decisions to ensure alignment with project goals."*

Question 220 | Soft Skills

How do you handle technical disagreements in a Python project ?

Answer

Suggested Answer Approach

- Emphasize data-driven decision-making (benchmarking, profiling).

- Highlight respectful discussions and willingness to consider alternative solutions.

- Mention how you document decisions for future reference.

Example statement: *"I handle technical disagreements by focusing on objective data. If there's a debate over performance, I benchmark both approaches and present results. I also ensure discussions remain respectful and collaborative."*

Question 221 | Soft Skills

How do you mentor junior Python developers ?

Answer

Suggested Answer Approach

- Discuss pair programming, code reviews, and knowledge-sharing sessions.

- Highlight the importance of guiding without micromanaging.

- Mention how you encourage best practices and continuous learning.

Example statement: *"I mentor junior developers through pair programming and structured code reviews. I encourage them to explore best practices while providing constructive feedback. My goal is to help them grow independently."*

Question 222 | Soft Skills

How do you handle burnout or maintain productivity in long-term Python projects ?

Answer

Suggested Answer Approach

- Discuss time management techniques (Pomodoro method, task batching).

- Highlight the importance of work-life balance and avoiding overcommitment.

- Mention strategies like automating repetitive tasks to reduce workload.

Example statement: *"I maintain productivity by using structured time management techniques and automating repetitive tasks. I also ensure work-life balance by setting realistic goals and taking breaks when needed."*

Question 223 | Soft Skills

How do you handle knowledge transfer when leaving a Python project ?

Answer

Suggested Answer Approach

- Mention comprehensive documentation (README, API specs, inline comments).

- Discuss handover meetings and mentoring junior developers.

- Highlight the importance of code clarity and maintainability.

Example statement: *"I ensure smooth knowledge transfer by maintaining clear documentation and conducting handover meetings. I also mentor team members to ensure continuity and minimize disruptions."*

Question 224 | Soft Skills

How do you ensure Python applications remain secure against vulnerabilities ?

Answer

Suggested Answer Approach

- Discuss secure coding practices (input validation, avoiding hardcoded secrets).

- Mention dependency scanning (pip-audit, bandit) and regular security reviews.

- Highlight authentication best practices (OAuth, JWT, bcrypt).

Example statement: *"I follow OWASP guidelines, conduct regular security audits, and use dependency scanning tools to detect vulnerabilities. Secure authentication and encryption ensure data protection."*

Question 225 | Soft Skills

How do you handle unexpected production issues in a application ?

Answer

Suggested Answer Approach

- Explain how you use logging, monitoring tools (Prometheus, New Relic), and error tracking (Sentry).

- Mention structured debugging techniques like rollback strategies and hotfix deployment.

- Highlight the importance of post-mortem analysis to prevent future occurrences.

Example statement: *"I handle production issues by first analyzing logs and monitoring alerts to pinpoint the root cause. I prioritize quick fixes while ensuring long-term solutions through post-mortem analysis and preventive measures."*

Question 226 | Soft Skills

How do you handle working with legacy Python code ?

Answer

Suggested Answer Approach

- Explain how you refactor code incrementally while ensuring backward compatibility.

- Mention writing tests before modifying legacy code to prevent regressions.

- Highlight the importance of understanding dependencies and gradual modernization.

Example statement: *"I approach legacy code by first writing tests to ensure stability before refactoring. I modernize incrementally while maintaining backward compatibility to avoid disruptions."*

Question 227 | Soft Skills

How do you handle situations where a project deadline is unrealistic ?

Answer

Suggested Answer Approach

- Explain how you assess feasibility and communicate concerns early.
- Mention strategies like breaking tasks into milestones or prioritizing critical features.
- Highlight how you negotiate with stakeholders to adjust scope or resources.

Example statement: *"I handle unrealistic deadlines by assessing feasibility and discussing adjustments with stakeholders. I prioritize critical features and suggest phased releases to ensure quality while meeting business needs."*

Question 228 | Soft Skills

How do you handle working with a difficult team member in a Python project ?

Answer

Suggested Answer Approach

- Explain how you focus on professionalism and collaboration.
- Mention strategies like active listening, clear communication, and finding common ground.
- Highlight how you escalate issues constructively if needed.

Example statement: *"I handle difficult team dynamics by maintaining professionalism and focusing on collaboration. Clear communication and active listening help resolve conflicts, and I escalate issues constructively if necessary."*

Question 229 | Soft Skills

How do you handle a situation where a stakeholder requests a last-minute change ?

Answer

Suggested Answer Approach

- Explain how you evaluate the impact and feasibility of the change.
- Mention how you communicate trade-offs and risks to stakeholders.
- Highlight strategies like feature toggles or incremental updates to minimize disruption.

Example statement: *"I assess last-minute changes based on feasibility and impact. I communicate trade-offs and suggest incremental updates to minimize disruption while meeting business needs."*

>>> The Psychology of Interviews

Technical interviews are more than just coding challenges, questions and answers, but they are psychological tests that assess problem-solving, communication, adaptability, and resilience.

Understanding the psychology behind technical interviews can help candidates prepare effectively, stay confident, and navigate the process strategically.

Why Do Companies Conduct Technical Interviews ?

Technical interviews are designed to evaluate

Problem-solving ability – How well candidates approach challenges.

Communication skills – Can they explain their thought process clearly ?

Adaptability – How do they handle unexpected questions or pressure ?

Collaboration – Can they work well with a team ?

Resilience – How do they react to failure or difficult problems ?

Common Psychological Challenges in Technical Interviews

Candidates often experience

- ★ **Imposter Syndrome** – Feeling unqualified despite having the skills.
- ★ **Performance Anxiety** – Fear of making mistakes under pressure.

★ **Cognitive Overload** – Struggling to think clearly due to stress.
★ **Fear of Rejection** – Worrying about failing the interview.

Pre-Interview Preparation – Setting Yourself Up for Success

Psychological Preparation Before the Interview

- **Adopt a Growth Mindset** – View interviews as learning experiences.

- **Practice Self-Compassion** – Accept that mistakes happen and focus on improvement.

- **Visualize Success** – Imagine yourself confidently solving problems.

- **Manage Stress** – Use deep breathing, meditation, or exercise.

Researching the Company and Role

- Understand the company's tech stack and engineering culture.
- Review common interview questions for the role.
- Study past interview experiences shared online.

Structured Reading for Offline Preparation

Instead of relying only on online coding platforms, focus on books and structured reading as well.

- **Cracking the Coding Interview** – Covers behavioral and technical questions.

- **Programming Interviews Exposed** – Explains problem-solving strategies.

- **Software Engineering Interview Series (Beyond The Invisible)** - Helps to prepare interviews as mockup, 3 – 4 days to review, designed to be Q&A guide.

- **Soft Skills – The Software Developer's Life Manual** – Focuses on career growth and communication.

- **The Psychology of Problem-Solving** – Helps develop structured thinking.

Mock Interviews Without Online Tools

- **Self-Practice** – Solve problems on paper, explaining solutions aloud.

- **Group Study** – Conduct mock interviews with peers.

- **Case Studies** – Analyze real-world interview experiences from books.

Understanding the Brain's Response to Interviews

The Neuroscience of Stress and Performance

Interviews trigger the **fight-or-flight response**, activating the **amygdala**, the brain's fear-processing center.

This can lead to

- Increased heart rate and sweaty palms.
- Difficulty recalling information due to cognitive overload.
- Impaired decision-making under pressure.

However, controlled stress can enhance focus and alertness. The key is regulating stress hormones like cortisol and adrenaline to maintain optimal performance.

The Role of Dopamine and Confidence

Dopamine, the reward neurotransmitter, plays a crucial role in confidence and motivation.

When dopamine levels are high, you experience

- Increased focus and mental clarity.
- Better memory recall and problem-solving ability.
- Higher resilience to setbacks.

Boosting dopamine before an interview can enhance cognitive function and reduce anxiety.

Pre-Interview Brain Optimization Techniques

Preparing for an interview isn't just about memorizing answers or studying technical concepts – it's about optimizing your brain's cognitive function, emotional resilience, and psychological readiness. Understanding how the brain processes stress, confidence, and problem-solving can help you perform at your best.

This chapter explores scientifically backed techniques to prepare your brain for an interview, covering neuroscience, cognitive psychology, and behavioral strategies.

Cognitive Priming: Training Your Brain for Success

What is Cognitive Priming ?

Cognitive priming is the process of **preloading your brain** with relevant information to improve recall and confidence. It works by activating neural pathways associated with problem-solving, memory, and verbal articulation before an interview.

When you prime your brain, you create a mental framework that makes it easier to retrieve information under pressure. This technique is widely used by athletes, public speakers, and high-performing professionals to enhance performance.

How Cognitive Priming Works in the Brain

The brain operates on associative memory, meaning it retrieves information based on patterns and connections. When you mentally rehearse interview scenarios, your brain strengthens the neural pathways related to those topics, making recall faster and more accurate.

For example, if you practice answering behavioral questions before an interview, your brain associates those responses with real-world experiences, making it easier to recall them when needed.

Techniques for Cognitive Priming

✓ **Mental Rehearsal** – Visualizing yourself answering questions confidently.
✓ **Memory Chunking** – Breaking down complex topics into smaller, manageable pieces.

✓ **Pattern Recognition** – Reviewing past interview questions to recognize common themes.

Example Exercise: Mental Rehearsal

1. Find a quiet space and close your eyes.

2. Visualize yourself walking into the interview room, greeting the interviewer, and sitting confidently.

3. Imagine answering questions smoothly, maintaining eye contact, and articulating responses clearly.

4. Repeat this process daily to reinforce positive mental associations.

Neuroplasticity and Learning Retention

What is Neuroplasticity?

Neuroplasticity is the brain's ability to adapt and reorganize itself by forming new neural connections. This means that consistent practice can rewire your brain to improve memory, problem-solving, and verbal articulation.

How Neuroplasticity Enhances Interview Performance

When you repeatedly engage with interview-related material, your brain strengthens the synaptic connections associated with those topics. This makes it easier to retrieve information quickly and apply knowledge effectively during the interview.

Techniques to Improve Learning Retention

✓ **Spaced Repetition** – Reviewing concepts at intervals to reinforce memory.

✓ **Active Recall** – Testing yourself instead of passively reading.

✓ **Interleaved Learning** – Mixing different topics to improve adaptability.

Example Exercise: Spaced Repetition

1. **Day 1:** Read a set of interview questions and answers.

2. **Day 3:** Review the same questions without looking at the answers.

3. **Day 7:** Test yourself again, focusing on recall accuracy.

4. **Day 14:** Repeat the process to solidify memory retention.

The Power of Sleep and Memory Consolidation

Why Sleep is Crucial for Interview Success

Sleep plays a critical role in memory consolidation, transferring information from short-term storage to long-term retention. Studies show that deep sleep enhances problem-solving ability, making it easier to recall information under pressure.

How Sleep Affects Cognitive Function

During sleep, the brain

✓ Strengthens neural connections related to learning.

✓ Clears out unnecessary information, improving focus.

✓ Enhances emotional regulation, reducing anxiety.

Optimizing Sleep for Interview Preparation

✓ **Aim for 7-9 hours of sleep** before an interview.

✓ **Avoid screens before bed** to prevent blue light disruption.

✓ **Use guided meditation** to improve sleep quality.

Example Exercise: Sleep Optimization Routine

1. **Set a consistent bedtime** to regulate circadian rhythms.

2. **Avoid caffeine and heavy meals** before sleep.

3. **Practice deep breathing** to relax the nervous system.

4. **Use a sleep journal** to track patterns and improve rest quality.

Emotional Regulation and Confidence Building

How Emotions Impact Interview Performance

The prefrontal cortex regulates emotions and logical thinking. Strengthening this area helps control interview anxiety and enhances decision-making ability.

Techniques for Emotional Regulation

✓ **Mindfulness Meditation** – Activates the prefrontal cortex, reducing stress.

✓ **Controlled Breathing** – Slows heart rate and calms the nervous system.

✓ **Cognitive Reframing** – Shifting negative thoughts into positive perspectives.

Example Exercise: Controlled Breathing

1. **Inhale deeply for 5 seconds**, hold for 2 seconds, and exhale for 7 seconds.

2. **Repeat this cycle for 5 minutes** to activate the parasympathetic nervous system.

3. **Use this technique before the interview** to maintain composure.

Power Posing and Body Language Psychology

How Body Language Influences Confidence

Your posture influences brain chemistry. Studies show that expansive body language increases testosterone (confidence hormone) and decreases cortisol (stress hormone).

Techniques for Power Posing

✓ **Stand tall with open posture** before the interview.

✓ **Use hand gestures** to reinforce confidence.

✓ **Maintain steady eye contact** to project authority.

Example Exercise: Power Posing Routine

1. Stand in a confident pose (hands on hips, shoulders back) for 2 minutes.

2. Take deep breaths to regulate stress hormones.

3. Walk into the interview with an upright posture, projecting confidence.

>>> **Hidden Gems**

Lesser-Known Libraries That Elevate Your Code

Python is packed with powerful standard libraries, but beyond the usual numpy, pandas, and requests, there exists a treasure trove of lesser-known libraries that bring efficiency, readability, and new possibilities to Python development. These gems help in data validation, CLI building, rich console output, async processing, and more.

1. Rich – Stunning Console Output

Purpose: Rich makes terminal output beautiful, adding color, tables, markdown rendering, and even interactive elements.

Why It's a Hidden Gem: Unlike the standard print() function, Rich makes terminal logs more readable with color, formatting, tables, progress bars, and even syntax highlighting for code.

```
from rich.console import Console
from rich.table import Table

console = Console()
table = Table(title="Python Hidden Gems")

table.add_column("Library", justify="center", style="cyan",
no_wrap=True)
table.add_column("Use Case", justify="center",
style="magenta")

table.add_row("Rich", "Beautiful Console Output")
table.add_row("Typer", "CLI Development")
```

```
table.add_row("Pydantic", "Data Validation")

console.print(table)
```

✓ Interactive tables

✓ Syntax highlighting

✓ Styled text with colors

2. Typer – The Easiest CLI Builder

Purpose: A minimalist, automatic command-line interface (CLI) builder based on Python's click module.

Why It's a Hidden Gem: Typer lets you create CLIs without writing extra boilerplate code, and it supports autocompletion and type annotations effortlessly.

Example

```python
import typer

app = typer.Typer()

@app.command()
def greet(name: str):
    """Greets the user"""
    typer.echo(f"Hello {name}!")

if __name__ == "__main__":
    app()
```

3. Pydantic – Robust Data Validation

Purpose: Pydantic makes data validation effortless, ensuring your Python models conform to expected formats.

Why It's a Hidden Gem: Unlike manually validating dictionary inputs, Pydantic parses, validates, and auto-casts data types, making API handling and configuration management smoother.

Example

```python
from pydantic import BaseModel

class User(BaseModel):
    name: str
    age: int

# Age is a string, but Pydantic will auto-convert
data = {"name": "Alice", "age": "25"}
user = User(**data)
print(user) # User(name='Alice', age=25)
```

4. Watchdog – File System Monitoring

Purpose: Watchdog listens for file system changes and reacts dynamically.

Why It's a Hidden Gem: Instead of constantly polling files, Watchdog watches file changes efficiently and triggers automated actions.

Example Code

```python
from watchdog.observers import Observer
from watchdog.events import FileSystemEventHandler

class MyHandler(FileSystemEventHandler):
```

```python
    def on_modified(self, event):
        print(f"File {event.src_path} has been modified")

observer = Observer()
observer.schedule(MyHandler(), path=".", recursive=True)
observer.start()
```

✓ Listens for **file changes** dynamically

✓ Supports **real-time automation**

✓ Works across **multiple operating systems**

5. PyFilesystem2 – Work with Filesystems Like Objects

Purpose: PyFilesystem2 provides an abstract filesystem API, allowing seamless interaction with local, remote, and cloud-based storage.

Why It's a Hidden Gem: Instead of directly managing file paths, it lets you treat filesystems like objects, whether you're working with S3, FTP, zip archives, or memory storage

Example

```python
import fs

home_fs = fs.open_fs('osfs://.')   # Works like an object!
print(home_fs.listdir('/')) # Ls files in the current dir
```

6. Poetry – Modern Dependency Management

Purpose: Poetry is a next-generation package manager that simplifies virtual environments and dependencies.

Why It's a Hidden Gem: Unlike pip and virtualenv, Poetry manages dependencies cleanly without requiring manual dependency resolution.

Code Level Gems

Argument Unpacking (*args and **kwargs) Beyond Basics

Understanding Argument Unpacking

In Python, *args and **kwargs allow functions to handle an arbitrary number of arguments dynamically. While many developers use them for basic argument passing, few realize their full potential in merging dictionaries, composing functions, and handling dynamic configurations.

Advanced Use Case - Dictionary Merging Without Loops

A hidden trick in Python allows dictionaries to be merged using **kwargs, eliminating the need for explicit loops:

```python
def merge_dicts(*dicts):
    return {**dicts[0], **dicts[1]}  # Efficient merging


data1 = {"name": "Alice", "age": 25}
data2 = {"city": "New York", "country": "USA"}


merged = merge_dicts(data1, data2)
print(merged)
# { Alice, 25, New York, USA }
```

Why This is Powerful

✓ Avoids manual iteration over dictionary keys.

✓ Python's internal dict merging is more efficient than explicit loops.

✓ Helps write concise code in API handling and config management.

Leveraging __missing__ for Custom Dictionary Behavior

What is __missing__?

__missing__ is a special method in Python's dict class that allows developers to define custom behavior for missing keys. Instead of using .get() or checking if key in dict, you can override dict behavior dynamically.

Example: Custom Default Dictionary Without .get()

```
class DefaultDict(dict):
    def __missing__(self, key):
        return f"Key '{key}' not found!"


data = DefaultDict({"name": "Alice"})
print(data["age"])   # Key 'age' not found!
```

Why This is Useful

✓ Avoids unnecessary if key in dict checks.

✓ Allows customized missing key behavior.

✓ Helps create dynamic lookup tables in data-heavy applications.

Using Ellipsis (...) for Multi-Dimensional Slicing

What is Ellipsis (...) ?

Most developers associate Ellipsis (...) with NumPy, but Python allows its use in slicing and custom objects, making it a powerful shortcut for multi-dimensional data handling.

Example: Flexible Slicing in Custom Objects

```python
class CustomSlice:
    def __getitem__(self, index):
        return f"Received slice: {index}"


obj = CustomSlice()
print(obj[1:5, ..., "test"])
```

Why This is Useful

✓ Allows **multi-dimensional indexing**, useful for AI/ML applications.

✓ Simplifies slicing operations for **data-heavy objects**.

✓ Avoids **manual tuple unpacking** for complex indexing.

Chaining Comparison Operators for Cleaner Code

Understanding Chained Comparisons

Instead of using multiple and conditions, Python allows chained comparisons, improving readability and logic clarity.

Example: Checking Value Ranges Without and

```python
x = 10
if 5 < x < 15:  # Equivalent to (5 < x) and (x < 15)
    print("x is within range")
```

Why This is Useful

✓ Removes redundant and conditions, making comparisons cleaner.

✓ Improves readability in validation and filtering logic.

Using with Statement for Automatic Resource Management

Why Use with ?

Python's with statement simplifies resource management, ensuring cleanup without requiring try-finally blocks.

Example: Automatic Cleanup in Custom Classes

```
class Resource:
    def __enter__(self):
        print("Resource acquired")
        return self

    def __exit__(self, exc_type, exc_value, traceback):
        print("Resource released")

with Resource():
    print("Using resource")
```

Why This is Useful

✓ Ensures clean resource handling without explicit cleanup logic.

✓ Prevents file locks, memory leaks, and database connection issues.

✓ Works well for file operations, threading, and database transactions.

Using functools.partial for Function Preloading

What is functools.partial ?

`partial()` allows preloading function arguments, making function calls more modular and reusable.

Example: Preloading Arguments for Reusable Functions

```python
from functools import partial

def power(base, exponent):
    return base ** exponent

square = partial(power, exponent=2)
print(square(5))  # 25
```

Why This is Useful

✓ Avoids lambda boilerplate for predefined arguments.

✓ Makes function calls more dynamic and reusable.

✓ Useful in command-line tools and functional programming.

Using dataclasses for Lightweight Objects

Why Use dataclasses ?

Instead of manually writing __init__, __repr__, and __eq__, Python's dataclass auto-generates these methods, reducing boilerplate.

Example: Auto-Generated Class Without Manual Methods

```python
from dataclasses import dataclass

@dataclass
class User:
    name: str
    age: int
```

```
user = User("Alice", 25)
print(user)  # User(name='Alice', age=25)
```

Why This is Useful

✓ Removes redundant class definitions, improving readability.

✓ Automatically adds equality checks and representation methods.

✓ Great for data-heavy applications and API responses.

>>> Index

>>> Core Python Concepts

1. What is the significance of indentation in Python syntax ?

2. What does Pythonic mean, and how can code be Pythonic ?

3. What are docstrings, and how do they contribute to Python's syntax ?

4. What is tuple unpacking ?

5. What is the difference between single quotes ' ' double quotes " " and triple quotes ''' ''' ?

6. What is the difference between implicit and explicit type conversion ?

7. What is the difference between shallow and deep copies ?

8. What is the purpose of the pass statement ?

9. What is the difference between is and == operators ?

10. What is LEGB rule ?

11. What are the different ways to format strings ?

12. What is the difference between del, pop(), and remove() when working with lists ?

13. What are keyword-only arguments ?

14. What is the difference between if-elif-else and match-case ?

15. What are custom exceptions ?

16. What is Global Interpreter Lock (GIL), and how does it affect multi-threading ?

17. What is the purpose of __init__.py file ?

18. What is the difference between Python's list and tuple ?

19. What is the purpose of Python's with statement ?

20. What is the difference between @staticmethod and @classmethod ?

21. What is the purpose of __repr__ method ?

22. What is the difference between del and garbage collection ?

23. What is the purpose of __name__ variable ?

24. What are dataclasses, and how do they improve code readability ?25.

What is the difference between __str__ and __repr__ methods ?

26. What are @static_method and @class_method ?

27. What are map, filter and reduce methods ?

28. What is memoization, and how can it optimize functions ?

29. What is monkey patching, and why should it be used cautiously ?

30. What are frozen dataclasses, and how do they enforce immutability ?

31. What are weak references, and how do they improve memory management ?

32. What are Magic methods ?

33. How does Python implement method resolution order (MRO), and why is it important ?

34. How does Python internally handle mutability, and what are its implications ?

35. What are Python's built-in functions ?

36. Why should you avoid using a blanket except: clause, and what are the risks ?

>>> Artificial Intelligence (AI)

37. How does Python enable generative AI for text, image, and code generation ?

38. How does PyTorch framework simplify advanced machine learning tasks ?

39. What are the differences between PyTorch and TensorFlow ?

40. How does Python facilitate Natural Language Processing (NLP) with libraries like spaCy and NLTK ?

41. What are the advantages of using FastAPI over Flask for AI model deployment ?

42. How can Python engineers ensure transparency in generative AI models ?

43. How does Python support ethical AI development through libraries and frameworks ?

44. What is the difference between pre-trained and fine-tuned models in generative AI ?

45. What are the key differences between PyTorch's dynamic computation graph and TensorFlow's static graph ?

46. What are tokenization techniques in NLP ?

47. What is model drift ?

48. What are attention mechanisms in deep learning, and why are they important ?

49. What is the difference between batch inference and real-time inference in AI model deployment ?

50. How do you ensure reproducibility in AI experiments ?

51. What is the difference between supervised and unsupervised learning ?

52. What are the main differences between discriminative and generative models in AI ?

53. How does reinforcement learning differ from supervised and unsupervised learning ?

54. What are transformer models, and why have they revolutionized NLP ?

55. What is zero-shot learning ?

56. What are ethical concerns associated with AI-based decision-making systems ?

57. What is model explainability ?

58. What are the key challenges in deploying AI models at scale, and how can they be addressed ?

59. How do Python-based AI models ensure data privacy in sensitive applications ?

60. What is differential privacy ?

61. How does AI optimize hyperparameter tuning, and what methods are commonly used ?

62. What are AI-powered retrieval-augmented generation (RAG) models ?

63. What is multimodal AI ?

64. What is AI-powered knowledge distillation ?

65. What are adversarial AI attacks ?

66. What are edge AI applications, and how do they differ from cloud-based AI models ?

67. How does AI contribute to sustainable energy optimization ?

68. What is AI model pruning ?

69. How does AI-driven sentiment analysis improve customer experience ?

70. What are AI-powered digital twins ?

>>> Data Analysis

71. What is Data Wrangling in Pandas, and why is it important ?

72. What is the difference between .loc[] and .iloc[] in Pandas ?

73. How does NumPy improve numerical computing efficiency ?

74. What is broadcasting in NumPy, and how does it work ?

75. How does Streamlit simplify interactive dashboard development ?

76. How does Streamlit simplify interactive dashboard development ?

77. How do you visualize time-series data with Matplotlib ?

78. How do you create interactive bar charts with Plotly ?

79. What are some common statistical functions in NumPy ?

80. How does NumPy handle broadcasting ?

81. How does Streamlit improve interactive visualization compared to Jupyter Notebooks ?

82. How do you create a grouped bar chart using Matplotlib ?

83. How do you optimize large-scale data operations in Pandas ?

84. How does NumPy enable faster matrix operations compared to native Python lists ?

85. How does .merge() differ from .join() in Pandas ?

86. What is .astype() in Pandas, and how does it optimize data processing ?

87. How does NumPy's einsum() improve performance over standard matrix multiplication ?

88. What is the difference between st.table() and st.dataframe() in Streamlit ?

89. What are the differences between .hist() and sns.kdeplot() for data

distribution visualization ?

90. How do you optimize Pandas operations for handling large datasets ?

>>> Advanced Python

91. What are type hints in Python, and how do they improve code reliability?

92. How do you create a custom decorator ?

93. What is the difference between function decorators and class decorators?

94. How do context managers in Python help manage resources effectively ?

95. How do you implement a custom context manager ?

96. How do metaclasses work, and when should you use them ?

97. What is static type checking ?

98. What are the benefits of using functools.wraps() in Python decorators ?

99. How do Python's @staticmethod and @classmethod decorators differ ?

100. What are the benefits of using static typing in Python, and how does MyPy assist with type checking ?

101. How does Python's typing system handle optional types ?

102. What are common use cases for function decorators ?

103. What are the differences between manual resource management and context managers ?

104. What are metaclasses ?

105. What are abstract base classes (ABCs) ?

106. How does introspection help in debugging and metaprogramming ?

107. What are covariance and contravariance in Python's type hints ?

108. Why should you avoid using mutable default arguments in functions ?

109. How does decorator chaining work, and what are common use cases ?

110. How do descriptor objects enhance class attribute management ?

111. What are weak references, and how do they help manage memory ?

112. How does Python handle monkey patching, and when should it be avoided ?

113. How does Python's method resolution order (MRO) affect class inheritance ?

114. What is the difference between runtime type checking and static type checking ?

115. Why __slots__ improve performance ?

116. Why should you use __slots__ in Python classes ?

>>> Async Programming and Real-Time Systems

117. What is an event loop in Python's asyncio, and why is it important ?

118. What is the difference between asyncio.gather() and asyncio.create_task() ?

119. What is await ?

120. How does aiohttp improve HTTP requests in asynchronous applications ?

121. What are WebSockets, and how do they enable real-time communication ?

122. How does Trio simplify asynchronous programming compared to asyncio ?

123. What are the key differences between traditional threading and async programming ?

124. What are structured concurrency principles, and how does Trio

implement them ?

125. What are cancellation tokens in asyncio, and how do they help manage async workflows ?

126. How does asyncio.Semaphore prevent resource overuse in concurrent async tasks ?

127. How do message queues enhance communication between asynchronous components ?

128. How do asyncio signals (loop.add_signal_handler()) improve real-time systems ?

129. How do backpressure handling techniques improve real-time streaming applications ?

130. How does Python's async IO model handle thousands of concurrent connections efficiently ?

131. What are async lifecycle hooks, and why are they important in real-time systems ?

132. Why does Python recommend using bounded async queues for high-performance systems ?

133. What are async watchdog timers, and how do they improve system reliability ?

>>> Concurrency and Parallelism

134. What is the difference between concurrency and parallelism ?

135. How does the Global Interpreter Lock (GIL) affect multithreading ?

136. What are the differences between threads, processes, and async tasks ?

137. How does multiprocessing overcome the limitations of the GIL ?

138. What are the advantages of using Dask for parallel computing ?

139. How does Ray improve distributed parallel computing compared to traditional multiprocessing ?

140. What is the difference between thread pools and process pools ?

141. How does Python support distributed parallel execution (Ray actors) ?

142. Why is it important to use multiprocessing.Queue() instead of queue.Queue() in parallel processes ?

143. What are lock-free data structures, and how do they improve parallel computing ?

144. What are the key differences between Python's asyncio and multi-threading for concurrency ?

145. What are real-world applications of parallel computing in Python ?

146. What are Ray tasks, and how do they enable parallel execution ?

147. How does Python handle inter-process communication (IPC) in parallel computing ?

148. What is False Sharing ?

149. How does cache line size affect false sharing in multi-threading ?

150. What is cache thrashing in multi-threaded applications, and how does it affect performance ?

151. What is priority inversion in multi-threaded applications, and how can it be prevented ?

>>> **Data Structures**

152. How does Python's list implement dynamic resizing, and what is its time complexity for appending elements ?

153. What is the difference between tuples and lists in Python, and when should you use tuples instead of lists ?

154. How do Python sets achieve constant-time lookup, and why are they faster than lists for membership testing ?

155. How do Python dictionaries implement key-value storage, and what is their average lookup time complexity ?

156. How do heaps (heapq) work in Python, and what are their practical applications ?

157. How does Python optimize dictionary (dict) key lookup operations ?

158. How does Python's OrderedDict differ from dict, and when should you use it ?

159. How does Python implement reference counting for memory management in data structures ?

160. How does Python handle memory fragmentation in dynamic data structures ?

161. How does Python handle memory fragmentation in dynamic data structures ?

>>> Data Engineering and Big Data

162. What is Apache Airflow ?

163. What is the difference between PySpark and Dask for Big Data processing ?

164. How does PySpark's DataFrame API optimize query execution compared to Pandas ?

165. How does PySpark handle partitioning in distributed computing, and

how does it improve performance ?

166. What is the difference between wide and narrow transformations in PySpark ?

167. How do you design a Data Lake architecture in the cloud, and what considerations affect storage, access, and governance ?

168. What is data modeling, and why is it important in Data Engineering ?

169. Explain the difference between structured data and unstructured data.

170. What are Big Data's four Vs, and why do they matter ?

171. What is the difference between a data warehouse and an operational database ?

172. Designing scalable ETL pipelines.

173. What are the three main types of data models ?

174. What is a Snowflake Schema ?

175. What is a Star Schema ?

176. What is Batch Processing ?

177. Explain the concept of data partitioning ?

>>> Cloud and DevOps

178. How do you ensure high availability and fault tolerance in Python-based cloud applications deployed on Kubernetes ?

179. What are the common challenges in developing networking applications, and how can they be addressed ?

180. How do Python-based DevOps workflows integrate with cloud monitoring and logging solutions to improve observability ?

181. How do you ensure continuous monitoring and auto-scaling for Python-

based applications in cloud environments ?

182. How does Kubernetes ensure container orchestration for Python applications, and what are its advantages ?

183. What is the difference between Continuous Integration (CI), Continuous Delivery (CD), and Continuous Deployment ?

184. How do you implement blue-green deployments in cloud environments, and why are they beneficial ?

185. How does Python integrate with cloud-native monitoring solutions like Prometheus and ELK Stack ?

186. What are some common tools used in DevOps for CI/CD pipelines ?

187. What is the difference between Virtual Machines (VMs) and Docker containers ?

>>> Security

188. How do you implement encryption in Python using PyCryptodome, and why is it essential for data protection ?

189. What are some real-life security incidents in Python applications, and how were they resolved ?

190. What is authentication in web applications ?

191. What is the difference between authentication and authorization, and why are both necessary for security ?

192. What is the difference between symmetric and asymmetric encryption ?

193. What are common API security vulnerabilities ?

194. What is the role of hashing in security ?

195. What is the principle of least privilege ?

196. How do you implement secure session management in Python web applications ?

197. How do you prevent timing attacks in Python applications, and why are they a security concern ?

198. How do you prevent brute-force attacks ?

199. How do you secure Python applications against man-in-themiddle (MITM) attacks, and why are they dangerous ?

200. How do you secure Python applications against SQL injection in NoSQL databases ?

>>> Optimization

201. What is the difference between time complexity and space complexity in Python optimization, and why are both important ?

202. How does Python's built-in data structures impact performance optimization, and when should you use lists, sets, or dictionaries ?

203. What is vectorization in Python, and how does it optimize numerical computations ?

204. What is loop unrolling ?

205. What is branch prediction ?

206. How does Python's numba library improve performance, and when should it be used ?

207. What is string interning, and how does it optimize performance ?

208. How does Python optimize integer storage using integer caching ?

209. What is Peephole optimization ?

210. What is Python's zero-cost exception handling ?

211. What is fast argument passing ?

212. What is __slots__ and how does it optimize attribute lookup ?

>>> Soft Skills

213. How do you handle debugging and troubleshooting complex Python issues ?

214. How do you collaborate with other developers in a project ?

215. What steps do you take to ensure code quality ?

216. How do you handle constructive criticism in code reviews ?

217. How do you handle unexpected project changes or shifting requirements ?

218. How do you handle working under tight deadlines ?

219. How do you handle ambiguity in project requirements ?

220. How do you handle technical disagreements in a Python project ?

221. How do you mentor junior Python developers ?

222. How do you handle burnout or maintain productivity in long-term Python projects ?

223. How do you handle knowledge transfer when leaving a Python project ?224. How do you ensure Python applications remain secure against vulnerabilities ?

225. How do you handle unexpected production issues in a application ?

226. How do you handle working with legacy Python code ?

227. How do you handle situations where a project deadline is unrealistic ?

228. How do you handle working with a difficult team member in a Python project ?

229. How do you handle a situation where a stakeholder requests a last-minute change ?

>>> The Psychology of Interviews

Common Psychological Challenges in Technical Interviews

Understanding the Brain's Response to Interviews

Neuroplasticity and Learning Retention

The Power of Sleep and Memory Consolidation

Emotional Regulation and Confidence Building

Power Posing and Body Language Psychology

>>> Hidden Gems

Power Posing and Body Language Psychology

Lesser-Known Libraries That Elevate Your Code

Code Level Gems

>>> BTS

The idea to create the series of software engineering book series emerged during one of the most crucial phases of my professional journey.

Like many others, I was seeking effective resources to prepare for technical interviews - a process that is often as daunting as it is essential. In my search, I scoured countless websites, forums, and blogs. While I did find some useful content, it was scattered across the internet like puzzle pieces, with no clear structure or logical order. Each platform offered its own unique chunks of information questions, tips, and insights, but the lack of coherence made studying a frustrating and inefficient task. I realized that if all of this invaluable information could be consolidated into one accessible, well-structured resource, it would not only make the preparation process smoother but also allow for a more focused and distraction-free experience. That's when I decided to create my own solution, a single, comprehensive collection of curated questions and guidance. A resource that could serve as a reliable companion for anyone preparing for interviews.

At first, this was a personal project. I started by assembling the content I had gathered, organizing it into meaningful sections and adding my own notes to fill in the gaps. The idea was simple, to create a study guide tailored to my needs, something I could rely on without jumping between tabs or losing track of what I had already covered. But as the project took shape, I began to realize its broader potential. If this approach was helping me, it could undoubtedly help others facing the same challenges, so it could help devs as well as programming enthusiasts to grasp between all areas of Python via reading this book and excel their knowledge.

While working on this, I also came to an important realization. Even the most advanced AI tools, while incredibly useful, often fall short in preparing candidates for interviews. These tools can assist in generating answers or explaining concepts, but true preparation demands more than just online assistance. It requires active engagement, off-screen practice, and the development of problem-solving skills that are essential in real-world scenarios.

And so, what began as a personal effort to streamline my own learning evolved into a mission, to create a book that could guide others through the complexities of interview preparation with clarity, structure, and purpose.

While preparing and crafting the book I have utilized a variety of advanced tools and technologies to make this book as comprehensive and helpful as possible.

Let's have a look at the main resources that played an important role.

★ **Microsoft Word**: Used for drafting, editing, and formatting the manuscript.

★ **Online Code Editors**: Utilized for writing and testing code snippets included in the book, ensuring they are functional and relevant.

★ **Adobe Illustrator**: Helped to create a visually appealing and professional book cover.

★ **Google Translate**: Ensured accurate translations and multilingual support, making the book accessible to readers worldwide.

★ **Microsoft Copilot**: This intelligent assistant was instrumental in generating and refining content, and ensuring the highest quality of questions and answers.

★ **Research Databases and Journals**: Extensive research was conducted using reputable databases and journals to ensure that the content was not only accurate but also aligned with the latest industry standards and practices.

★ **Amazon KDP (Kindle Direct Publishing)**: Helped for publishing and distributing the book, making it accessible to readers across the globe.

Author's Experience

Beyond the tools and technologies, the author's personal journey played a significant role in shaping this book. With years of experience in passing and conducting technical interviews, the author brings a unique perspective to the table. This firsthand experience ensures that the questions and answers are not only theoretically sound but also practically relevant.

Additionally, the author's role in conducting interviews has given him valuable insights into what employers look for in candidates.

These insights are woven throughout the book, offering readers a comprehensive understanding of both sides of the interview process.

Scan this QR code to access example questions from the book! 📖 ✦
Get insights, practice exercises, and key discussion topics directly from your device.

We Value Your Feedback! 🌟

Dear Reader,
Thank you for choosing to read this book.
Your support means the world to us!

If you found this book helpful in your interview preparation or if it sparked your interest in new topics, we would love to hear from you. Please consider leaving a review on Amazon.

Your feedback not only helps us improve but also assists other readers in finding valuable resources. Your honest review will make a significant difference.

Thank you for your time and support!

Warm regards,
Gleamixie

Made in United States
North Haven, CT
29 June 2025

70188009R00130